UKRAINE–NATO RELATIONS AND NEW PROSPECTS FOR PEACEKEEPING

Leonid Polyakov

THE ROYAL INSTITUTE OF INTERNATIONAL AFFAIRS | Russia and Eurasia Programme

Published in Great Britain in 2003
by the Royal Institute of International Affairs,
Chatham House, 10 St James's Square, London SW1Y 4LE
(Charity Registration No. 208 223)

Distributed worldwide by the Brookings Institution,
1775 Massachusetts Avenue, NW, Washington, DC 20036-2188

ISBN 1 86203 141 X

Cover design by Matthew Link
Typesetting in ITC Giovanni by Koinonia, Manchester
Printed and bound in Great Britain by the Chameleon Press Ltd

Dedicated to my long-time friend
Lieutenant-Colonel Peter Kanana,
who made a tremendous contribution
in laying the groundwork for successful
Ukraine–NATO military cooperation,
but whose devotion and enthusiasm
were not always adequately
recognized and valued.

CONTENTS

ABOUT THE AUTHOR

Leonid I. Polyakov is Director (Military Programmes) at the Ukrainian Centre for Economic and Political Studies, named after Olexander Razumkov (the Razumkov Centre), in Kiev. Previously, Col. Polyakov (Ukrainian Army retd.) served as State Expert, National Security and Defence Council Staff, Ukraine. He is a graduate of the US Army War College (1995), George C. Marshall Centre for European Security (2001) and Frunze Military Academy (Moscow, 1993).

ACKNOWLEDGMENTS

I am grateful to many people for their help with this book. This volume is the result of my own research collaboration with friends and colleagues from the Razumkov Centre – Dr Anatoliy Grytsenko, Dr Mykola Sungurovskiy and Dr Mikhail Pashkov, as well as Andriy Bychenko, Valeri Chaly and Liudmila Shanghina – to whom I am greatly indebted.

I thank the following people for providing assistance in formulating ideas and for their various contributions throughout the period of this work: Dr Andrej Karkoshka (Poland), Col. Harry Simmeth (US Army retd.), Dr Larry Black and Dr Natalie Mychajlyszyn (Canada), James Sherr (UK), Velentyn Badrak and Serhiy Zgurets (Ukraine).

Important portions of this book were influenced by my work as a NATO–EAPC research fellow in 1999–2001, which was made possible through a NATO award.

I am grateful to the Royal Institute of International Affairs at Chatham House, in particular Dr Roy Allison, Head of the Russia and Eurasia Programme, and James Nixey, Programme Coordinator, for their continuous support and encouragement during the preparation of this book.

I should also like to thank Gillian Bromley and the Razumkov Centre's intern Bohdanna Diduch, whose invaluable help in preparing the text for publication is greatly appreciated.

The views expressed in this volume are those of the author alone.

December 2002 L.P.

ABBREVIATIONS AND ACRONYMS

AOR	Area of Responsibility
CFE	Conventional Armed Forces in Europe
CFSP	[EU] Common Foreign and Security Policy
CIS	Commonwealth of Independent States
COMKFOR	Commander of Allied Forces in Kosovo
EAPC	Euro-Atlantic Partnership Council
ESDP	[EU] European Security and Defence Policy
GU[U]AM	Georgia, Ukraine, [Uzbekistan], Azerbaijan and Moldova
IFOR	Implementation Force
JWGDR	Joint Working Group on Defence Reform
KFOR	Kosovo Force
MEDEVAC	Medical Evacuation
MNB	Multinational Brigade (KFOR)
NACC	North Atlantic Cooperation Council
NATO	North Atlantic Treaty Organization
OSCE	Organization for Security and Cooperation in Europe
PARP	planning and review process [within PfP]
PCA	Partnership and Cooperation Agreement
PfP	Partnership for Peace [Programme]
SFOR	Stabilization Force [in the Former Yugoslavia]
SHAPE	Supreme Headquarters Allied Powers Europe
SOFA	Status of Forces Agreement
UNHCR	United Nations High Commissioner for Refugees

INTRODUCTION

NATO has an understandable interest in Ukraine, which has a considerable military, agricultural and industrial potential and a population of some 50 million. Ukraine borders the new NATO members Poland and Hungary, and two aspirants to membership – Slovakia and Romania; it also lies very close to an 'old' NATO country – Turkey. Ukraine not only remains an island of stability in a potentially volatile strip of 'conflict zones' through southern Europe, the Caucasus and Central Asia, but represents a cornerstone of stability in the broader European region. Mutually beneficial cooperation between Ukraine and NATO, therefore, is not only in the interest of the two parties in question, but is also important for overall European security. NATO views independent Ukraine as an integral part of Europe with ambitions to approach Western standards of political and economic performance, particularly in building its national security system, including border controls and intelligence and law-enforcement bodies, and in making a significant contribution to stability and security in the European region.

The development of Ukraine's cooperation with NATO is conditioned, in the first place, by the need to strengthen the external guarantees of Ukraine's national security. On the one hand, Ukraine's *rapprochement* with NATO is an important element of progress towards its integration into European structures, a strategic choice which is viewed with understanding and support by Ukraine's Western partners. On the other hand, the deepening of cooperation with NATO is not welcomed by Ukraine's strategic partner to the east – Russia. Russia's outright opposition, until very recently, to NATO's enlargement through the incorporation of central and east European countries presented a serious impediment to the development of Ukraine's relations with the alliance; and it is very likely that such an attitude will persist, despite Russia's cooperation with the anti-terrorist campaign mounted after 11 September 2001.

In the final analysis, the deepening of cooperation with NATO exerts a significant positive impact on Ukraine's security and serves its national interests. One of the major areas of this Ukraine–NATO cooperation – in terms of the scale of military-to-military contacts, money contributed, people engaged and practical cooperation in the field – is peacekeeping. The potential for cooperation between Ukraine and NATO in this area is quite significant and far exceeds the level attained so far. The alliance remains receptive to positive interaction; and a corresponding openness on Ukraine's part was confirmed in May 2002 when the leadership in Kiev finally announced that the country intends to join the alliance in the future.

The prospects for mutually beneficial cooperation are sound. The alliance is interested in a strong, democratic and independent Ukraine, which could become an even more important player in regional security efforts through participation in peacekeeping under the auspices of the

European Union's Security and Defence Policy (ESDP), which is close to NATO, or through revitalizing (within the framework of NATO's Partnership for Peace programme) the peacekeeping agenda within the GUUAM group (Georgia, Ukraine, Uzbekistan, Azerbaijan and Moldova), which is currently frozen as a result of Russian pressure. Whether Ukraine will be able fully to realize these potentials depends first and foremost on its own policies.

This paper consists of five chapters. Chapter 1 presents a general outline and provides data on the history and the current state of relations between Ukraine and NATO, as well as on the results of public and expert opinion polls on Ukraine–NATO relations. Chapter 2 focuses on one of the most influential elements in the relationship between Ukraine and NATO, Russia. Chapter 3 provides analysis of and information on practical peacekeeping-related activity within the framework of cooperation between Ukraine and NATO. Some of the important lessons learned – both practical and educational – are discussed. Chapter 4 relates the history of Ukrainian attempts to promote a peacekeeping agenda within GUUAM under the auspices of the PfP, and also touches upon the prospects of NATO–EU cooperation over peacekeeping and its possible implications for Ukraine. Overall, chapters 1 and 2 address the broad theme of Ukraine–NATO relations, while chapters 3 and 4 address the general topic of new prospects for peacekeeping. Finally, chapter 5 presents some general conclusions.

1 UKRAINE–NATO RELATIONS: WHAT IS AT ISSUE?

Brief history

During the first years after Ukraine became independent in 1991 the country's relations with NATO gradually became more institutionalized; however, they existed mainly in form rather than in substance, limited in effect to high-level meetings. In 1992 NATO secretary-general Manfred Wörner visited Kiev, and President Leonid Kravchuk of Ukraine visited Brussels; Ukrainian representatives began to participate actively in the work of the North Atlantic Cooperation Council (NACC). In 1993 further visits and consultations took place. In February 1994 Ukraine became the first country of the Commonwealth of Independent States (CIS) to join the NATO PfP programme, and later that year it participated in several PfP field exercises and sent a liaison officer to the Partnership Coordination Cell in Mons, Belgium (the Supreme Headquarters Allied Powers Europe – SHAPE). In June 1995 Kravchuk's successor as president, Leonid Kuchma, visited NATO headquarters in Brussels and proposed a 'special relationship' between Ukraine and NATO. This proposal led to a joint press statement on 14 September 1995 announcing that NATO and Ukraine had 'agreed to cooperate in the further strengthening of Ukraine–NATO relations across a broad front, including the development of an enhanced relationship both within and outside the PfP Programme and NACC activities'.

The same year, 1995, was the first year of Ukraine–NATO cooperation in a peacekeeping operation: IFOR, the international force in the former Yugoslavia, which has continued to the present, augmented in its later manifestations as SFOR and, later, KFOR (see Chapter 3 below).

On 9 July 1997, in Madrid, Ukraine and NATO signed a Charter on a Distinctive Partnership between the North Atlantic Treaty Organization and Ukraine. This event was a watershed in Ukraine–NATO relations. It provided a solid basis for further cooperation, in the first instance through the NATO–Ukraine Commission established by the charter. It also paved the way for the creation of a Joint Working Group on Defence Reform and a Joint Group on Civil Emergency Planning. Soon after signing the charter, NATO opened an Information and Documentation Centre in Kiev – the first on the territory of the former USSR – and established a NATO liaison office in Ukraine's ministry of defence (officially inaugurated on 28 November 2001). For its part, Ukraine placed representatives in NATO headquarters in Brussels (an ambassador and two-star general with a small staff) and in SHAPE in Mons (two liaison officers); ratified the Status of Forces Agreement (SOFA) and the 'open skies' treaties; and offered its large Yavoriv training centre in western Ukraine for the purposes of PfP exercises, particularly for peacekeeping.

While there are provisions for crisis consultations between Ukraine and NATO, they certainly fall well short of the military defence obligations listed in article 5 of the NATO Treaty, which apply to NATO members alone. NATO has not extended any security guarantees to Ukraine, but it has offered the country many opportunities for strengthening its security. In particular, the United States has provided Ukraine with millions of dollars in military aid, has partly subsidized Ukraine's participation in the PfP Programme through the Warsaw Initiative and has also contributed to supporting Ukrainian peacekeepers in the Balkans (Kosovo) through particular programmes of technical assistance.

Initially, however, Ukraine did not take effective advantage of these opportunities, its leaders tending to bite off more than they could chew. Over the period 1996–9, Ukraine planned to take part in around 300 PfP events in total (see figure 1), mainly conducted by the ministry of defence, but it actually participated in only half that number, as the necessary organizational capacity appeared to be beyond the country's capabilities. It was difficult to prepare the necessary documents, find the right people and allocate expenses (in those instances when NATO requested the Ukrainian side to cover at least part of the costs).

Nevertheless, cooperation within the PfP framework slowly but gradually became more productive. For instance, by the year 2000, the Ukrainian ministry of defence, which in 1995/6 employed just one officer to deal with NATO, operated an entire department staffed with qualified officers. Designated departments were also organized within the ministry of internal affairs, as well as other agencies. It should be noted that today, in contrast to much of the past, few events fail solely because of the Ukrainian side. From 2000 to 2002, the

Figure 1: Dynamics of Ukraine's defence cooperation with NATO

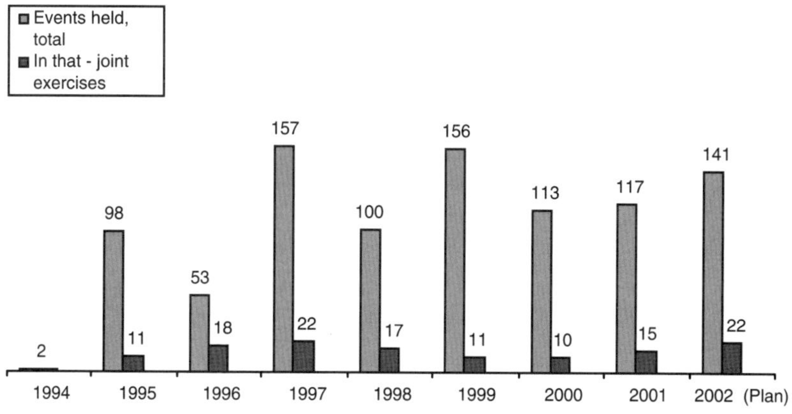

number of events, at least for Ukraine's military, has no longer been a goal in itself; there has been better prioritization, with a focus on strengthening national defence and improving interoperability with NATO .

Certainly, the progress of Ukraine–NATO relations was adversely affected by Ukrainian internal factors, among them uncertain public opinion, the absence of a common position among the political elite with respect to Ukraine's geopolitical orientation between Russia and the West (including NATO), the slow path of economic reform and delays in conducting defence reform.

Until 2002, there was no consensus in Ukraine about the country's future relations with the alliance. According to a public opinion poll carried out in June 2000 by the Razumkov Centre, only 10.5% of Ukrainians believed in NATO's desire to defend Ukraine in the event of aggression, or the threat of aggression. Slightly more than a third (37.5%) of respondents believed that NATO would defend Ukraine if it were a member of the alliance, while roughly the same number (36.9%) thought that it would not.[1] In this context, the population's position regarding Ukraine's possible accession to NATO was clear. Half (50.6%) of respondents in 2000 considered that Ukraine should never join NATO, a quarter (23.4%) said that it should join the alliance in five to ten years' time, and 9.3% of those polled responded that Ukraine should join NATO within ten to fifteen years.

It is interesting to compare these data with the opinion of Ukrainian experts questioned at a February 2000 'round table'. The experts, most of whom were drawn from the highest echelons of the executive and legislative branches of government, along with leading scholars in the field of national security, responded as follows: 41% said Ukraine should never join NATO; 15% said Ukraine should join NATO in five to ten years; 44% said it should join in ten to fifteen years. Many of the experts are likely to have visited the West, maybe frequently, and as a consequence to be better aware of the potential benefits to be derived from NATO membership than other segments of the Ukrainian population.

The picture that emerged was that in 2000, even after the allied operation in Kosovo, which was unpopular in

[1] See A. Bychenko and L. Polyakov, 'How much of NATO do Ukrainians want?', *Dzerkalo Tyzhnia*, 1 July 2000.

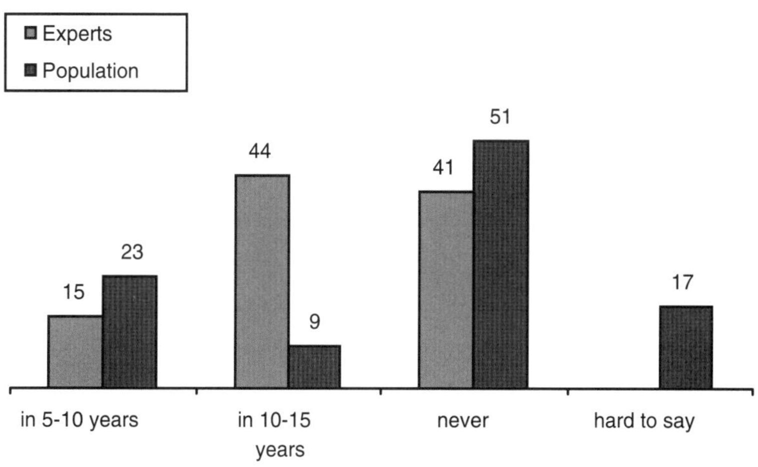

Ukraine, almost two-thirds (59%) of the country's elite and one-third (32.7%) of its population supported NATO membership (see figure 2). If NATO had been more successful in enforcing peace in the Balkans, and the process of EU enlargement did not threaten to cut Ukrainians off from the West, this percentage would probably have been higher still.

Superficially, the situation looked paradoxical. Ukraine did not have so high a level of military cooperation with any other international structure, which benefited it both politically and economically. But almost every second Ukrainian was critical of NATO.

There are several reasons why Ukrainians had a

negative attitude to NATO. The first is the persistence of conservative–nostalgic sentiments held by a certain element of the population – the 'legacy' of Soviet-era anti-NATO propaganda. The second revolved around Russia, whose relations with NATO remained tense (particularly concerning the question of the alliance's enlargement) at the same time as Russian influence over Ukraine strengthened; and the Russian mass media had a strong presence in Ukraine. Third, most Ukrainians were un-aware of the specific features of Ukraine's cooperation with NATO, particularly within the framework of the PfP. Almost two-thirds of respondents to the public opinion poll cited above (64.4%) either did not know anything at all about the programme, or did not know that Ukraine was a participant. Western information about NATO did not reach the grassroots level in Ukraine.

The fourth reason is the attitude of Ukrainians to the alliance's peace enforcement operation in the Balkans (particularly the fact that Ukraine's views were not taken into account). Most Ukrainians (56.6%) were convinced that, without UN authorization, NATO had no right to intervene in the internal affairs of Yugoslavia and its successor states, even to resolve humanitarian problems.

Notwithstanding these popular reservations, Ukraine still had one of the largest programmes of cooperation with NATO among all twenty-seven of the alliance's partner countries. According to unofficial estimates, the Ukraine–NATO cooperation programme was (and still is) three to four times as large any other similar pro-gramme between NATO and one of its partner countries (except, maybe, for the participants in the Membership

Action Plan[2]). It is the only participant of the PfP, apart from Russia, with which NATO maintains relations of 'distinctive partnership'.

Apart from joint cooperation on purely defensive issues, NATO has helped Ukraine significantly in the development of the legislative basis and implementation of democratic civilian control of the military sector and assisted with the adaptation to civilian life of retired servicemen; it supports the activity of non-governmental research organizations and Ukrainian scholars, and gives assistance in information technology and other technical areas. Cooperation with NATO in dealing with the aftermath of natural disasters and technological accidents also brought noticeable results. With NATO support (and to an extent depending on its available capabilities), Ukraine has taken part in strengthening stability and security in the European region. In addition to active military contacts within the PfP framework, Ukraine has cooperated with NATO in the Kosovo and Macedonian peacekeeping operations.

Thus, by 2000, Ukraine was in an uncomfortable situation: politically, primarily orientated towards the West and NATO, but economically heavily dependent on Russia. To complicate the situation, Ukraine's internal politics were becoming unbalanced, a situation precipitated by a rigid and corrupt political system, weak democratic institutions, growing impatience on the part of Western-oriented democratic reformers and a largely

[2] The Membership Action Plan is a set of measures agreed between NATO and a country which has applied for NATO membership, aimed at improving the candidate country's compatibility with NATO entry criteria.

passive population that was largely pessimistic about the prospect of integration with the West, especially in the south-eastern (pro-Russian) part of Ukraine.

Another complication was the country's inconsistent foreign policy, which suffered from attempts to sustain equally good relations with partners following diverse security agendas – the EU, the United States, Poland, Russia and NATO, for example. Overall, Ukraine found itself more dependent and less secure between growing pressure from both West and East. As one prominent Ukrainian political scientist described the situation:

> The strategic dependence [of Ukraine] on much more powerful nations, especially those whose relations with each other are complicated, unpredictable, and laden with all the elements of rivalry … not so much secures against unwanted relationships, as excludes the possibility to develop cooperation with desirable partners in advantageous spheres and forms.[3]

However, it was clear that, in the long run, objective Ukrainian interests and the basic values of the majority of its population would ultimately drive Kiev closer to the West and NATO.

For its part, NATO had constantly reiterated its interest in Ukraine: 'Its size and pivotal geostrategic role make Ukraine a key to ensuring Europe's long-term stability. That is why NATO has consistently sought to assist Ukraine, as it charts its way into the future.'[4]

[3] O. Dergachov, 'Determinants and illusions of strategic partnership', *National Security and Defence*, no. 12, 2000, pp. 70–73.
[4] G. Robertson, speech delivered at the Ukraine–NATO symposium, 'The world in the 21st century: cooperation, partnership, dialogue'; see *http://www.nato.int*.

Recent developments

A new development in Ukraine–NATO relations was signalled by NATO Secretary-General George Robertson's statement that 'cooperative ventures of Ukraine and NATO are intended to complement Ukraine's wider process of reform. They are a clear expression of the Alliance's determination not to leave Ukraine alone as it charts its course into the future.'[5]

At the especially difficult time for NATO that followed the 11 September terrorist attacks on the United States, Ukraine unconditionally supported the alliance. The statement by the NATO–Ukraine Commission of 12 September 2001 reads: 'NATO and Ukraine condemn in the strongest possible terms these atrocities, and stand united in their commitment to ensure that those responsible are brought to justice and punished. In the spirit of its distinctive partnership with NATO, Ukraine stands ready to contribute fully to this effort.'[6] During the meeting of the NATO–Ukraine Commission in ambassadorial session on 22 October 2001, the NATO allies 'expressed their appreciation of Ukraine's decision to open its airspace for overflight by US aircraft, and its statement that it believed NATO's invocation of Article 5 in response to the attacks to be completely valid'.[7] By the end of summer 2002, Ukraine's airspace had been overflown by more than three thousand NATO planes in support of the anti-terrorist operation in Afghanistan. In at least one

[5] Ibid.

[6] See statement by the NATO–Ukraine Commission, NATO press release 126, 14 Sept. 2001.

[7] See statement by the NATO–Ukraine Commission, NATO press release 142, 22 Oct. 2001.

case, an emergency landing was requested and granted. Access to Ukrainian airspace was supplemented by other modest cooperative efforts – for instance, Ukraine and the United States signed a contract worth $40 million to supply 2 million Ukrainian gas masks to the United States.[8]

The NATO–Ukraine Commission also underlined the general improvement of bilateral cooperation.[9] Special attention was paid to 'the substantial progress' made by the NATO–Ukraine Joint Working Group on Defence Reform (JWGDR). In 2001 the JWGDR achieved meaningful progress in cooperation within six identified areas: rationalization of defence structures; professionalization; reform of border troops; reform of internal security forces; reduction of mobilization resources and stockpiles; and democratic civilian control.

Indeed, despite continued complaints from NATO headquarters that Ukraine often makes decisions but fails to implement them (especially on the issue of Ukraine's arms trade with Macedonia – an issue of major controversy between Ukraine and NATO in 2001),[10]

[8] 'Ukraine will supply to the USA 2 million gas masks', *Defense-Express*, 3 Dec. 2001; see *http://www.defence-ua.com*.

[9] See statement by the NATO–Ukraine Commission, NATO press release 142, 22 Oct. 2001. 'The NATO–Ukraine Commission also underlined the substantial enhancement of NATO–Ukraine cooperative activities in defense reform, military cooperation, science, technology, environmental protection, economics and civil emergency planning. Ambassadors commended the work of both the NATO Information and Documentation Centre and the NATO Liaison Office in Kiev, and agreed to actively support them in fulfilling their respective missions.'

[10] 'Ukraine often makes decisions but fails to implement them – NATO representative', *Defense-Express*, 4 Dec. 2001; see *http://www.defence-ua.com*.

Ukraine–NATO relations improved perceptibly in 2001. This is illustrated by the following developments: an accord between NATO and Ukraine on converting the air force base at Uzyn (70 kilometres from Kiev) for peaceful use; the implementation of a NATO PFP Trust Fund, supported by Canada, Hungary and Poland, aimed at supporting Ukraine in the destruction of 400,000 anti-personnel landmines; and the award of some 300 scientific grants to Ukrainian scholars in 2001. By the end of the year there had been numerous declarations by Ukrainian foreign and security policy officials on the need further to strengthen ties between Ukraine and NATO, through the modernization (by which was meant extension) of the 1997 charter.

Finally, in May 2002, Ukraine's leadership decided to seek to develop a more ambitious and binding framework of cooperation with NATO. It declared the strategic goal of joining the alliance, and askd NATO to recognize Ukraine as a prospective member. According to Ukraine's foreign minister, there are two important reasons for Ukraine's search for clarity about its prospects of membership. 'First, because it will allow us to focus relevant resources on achieving the required criteria … Second, because it will mean recognition of Ukraine as a European state. Recognition, which we still lack in our relations with the European Union.'[11]

In forming a picture of present circumstances it is important to note that the positive shift in the Ukrainian

[11] See address by Minister Anatoly Zlenko at the NATO–Ukraine Charter 5th anniversary international conference, 'NATO–Ukraine: main achievements and prospects for mutual relations', Kiev, 9 July 2002.

leadership's attitude to NATO coincides with a corresponding change in how ordinary Ukrainians see the alliance. According to opinion polls conducted by the Razumkov Centre in spring/summer 2002, the image of NATO in the eyes of Ukrainian citizens, which had deteriorated markedly after the alliance's operation in Kosovo, is improving considerably. There are signs that official and grassroots positions on relations with NATO are converging, in contrast to the results of previous opinion polls.

By the middle of 2002, the number of respondents who believed NATO to be an aggressive military bloc had declined sharply in comparison with one or two years before (from 48.1% in 2001 to 32.6% in 2002). The number of those who regarded NATO as a defensive alliance had grown slightly and the number of those who believed it to be a peacekeeping organization remained the same. But the number of respondents who found it difficult to characterize the alliance definitely grew markedly – by a third. This uncommitted section of Ukrainian opinion may be a potential reservoir of support for NATO.

Evidently, the overall Ukrainian attitude to NATO has changed radically: in marked contrast to the earlier poll, more people than before view it positively rather than negatively (37.4% in 2002 against 32.6% in 2001). One of the principal reasons for this change was a positive psychological response to the successful operation in Afghanistan led by NATO's leading power – the United States. Allied countries were seen as proving their ability to use their high combat potential and to act flexibly in the international arena. It is also important that Ukraine and, especially, Russia took an active part in the anti-terrorist coalition. The common fight against terrorism significantly improved Russia's relations with the United States and NATO. Moreover, an increasing number of Ukrainians support the idea of Ukraine's integration with the EU, the backbone of which is made up of NATO member countries.

It can also be expected that Ukraine's *rapprochement* with NATO will be supported by the new Ukrainian parliament elected on 31 March 2002. According to the returns of a February 2002 poll among leaders of political parties and blocs, the majority of those who were elected to parliament (except delegates of the Communist Party) agreed on the expediency of Ukraine's membership in NATO.

What form should the Ukraine–NATO relationship take? The experience of Ukraine's neighbours to the west shows that there is no rational alternative now for Kiev to strengthening its cooperation with the alliance. Ukrainians' view of this problem has also changed lately. Their assessments are summarized in figure 3. The most notable change is the drastic reduction (from 45.6% to 28.4%) since 2000 in the number of those who support Ukraine's non-aligned status. There are grounds for inferring that Ukraine's non-alignment is widely regarded currently as an expression of uncertainty and vagueness in foreign policy, as keeping aloof from global and European processes.

However, despite a general growth in the desire of Ukrainians to join NATO, Ukraine's formal accession to

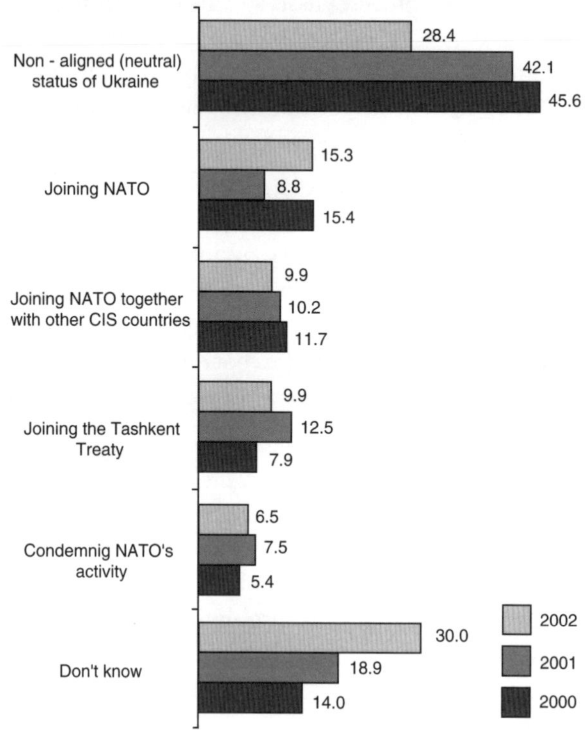

the alliance in the near future does not seem a very
realistic aim. This is not just a matter of Ukraine's inten-
tions, but of its ability to ensure compliance with NATO
membership criteria, and of the real economic capabilities of the state. If the economic potential of Ukraine is
compared to that of the new NATO members (Poland,

Hungary and the Czech Republic), with roughly equal indicators of aggregate territory, population and the strength of armed forces, then Ukraine is seen to lag behind significantly in terms of GDP and defence expenditures. Moreover, one should remember that the new members of the alliance have been consistently criticized over the extent of their compliance with NATO standards, in particular for insufficient defence expenditure.[12]

The question of Ukraine's commitment to NATO remains even after the recent declarations of intent to join NATO. Chief among current priorities for Ukraine–NATO relations is the tally of eighty national defence reform objectives, jointly developed by Ukraine and NATO, and approved by Ukraine's minister of defence together with nineteen NATO nations. Its aim is to strike a finite balance between defence plans and defence resources in the best interests of the state. However, there is still no guarantee that Ukraine will successfully implement these objectives. There is also a question of consistency between the declared and real policy of Ukraine with respect to political and economic development. To be accepted as a prospective candidate, Ukraine needs to show real achievements in embedding democracy – by checking corruption, allowing more freedom of expression and strengthening civil society.

There is also the problematic factor of Russia, which, despite its recent *rapprochement* with NATO, continues to oppose the alliance's enlargement.[13] Russia's position in

[12] See A. Karkoszka, 'Following in the footsteps', *NATO Review*, Spring 2002, *http://www.nato.int/docu/review/2002/issue1/art4.html*.
[13] See e.g. D. Trenin, 'Silence of the bear', *NATO Review*, Spring 2002, *http://www.nato.int/docu/review/2002/issue1/art3.html*: 'The "silence of

its dialogue with NATO is quite strong, as it has not only
become an important ally in the campaign against terrorism since 11 September, but remains a nuclear power, a
key participant in arms control regimes and a major
supplier of energy resources to Europe.

.

the bear" should not be misinterpreted in the West among hopes for
a "new beginning". The bulk of Russia's political establishment, particularly the foreign, defence and security communities, still resent what
some refer to as NATO's "eastern march", because it erodes their self-
esteem and the traditional notion of Russia as a great power.'

2 UKRAINE–NATO RELATIONS THROUGH THE PRISM OF THE RUSSIAN FACTOR

Analysis of the impact of the Russian factor on Ukraine's relations with NATO shows that Russia still considers Ukraine and NATO to be pursuing policies damaging to Russia's interests in several areas. Until recently Russia consistently put pressure on Ukraine to reduce its cooperation with NATO. So far this has not achieved any visible success. The major reasons for this are as follows: most Ukrainians do not regard themselves as either Russians or 'little' Russians, contrary to what the majority of Russians are accustomed to believe; Russia's pretensions to dominance in the region preclude equality in relations between Russia and Ukraine, which is hardly accommodating to Ukrainians; and because there is still no confidence between the two countries, there is no viable basis for especially close security cooperation.

Brief history

In the decade between Ukraine becoming independent in 1991 and Russia electing a new president in March 2000, the presence of the Russian factor in relations between NATO and Ukraine went through three stages.[1]

[1] The content of this section is based on research conducted by the author within the framework of the NATO–EAPC Fellowship Programme 1999–2001. The subject of the research was 'The Russian factor in Ukraine's relations with NATO: possible outcomes and policy implications for Ukraine and NATO'.

During the first period, from Ukraine's gaining independence in 1991 until 1995, Russia was forming its policy towards Ukraine and NATO, and waiting for Ukraine to fall back within the Russian sphere of influence. The second period, from 1996 to 1998, could be called a period of Russian suspicion towards growing Ukraine–NATO cooperation, when Russia also cooperated with NATO and struggled to achieve a relationship of equals with the alliance, but simultaneously objected to the development of cooperation between NATO and Ukraine. The third period, from early 1999 till early 2000, was a period of open Russian hostility towards Ukraine–NATO cooperation, during which in many ways Russian cooperation with NATO regressed.

Between 1992 and 1995, Russia and leading NATO countries were preoccupied with the denuclearization of Ukraine, and with supporting the emerging democracy in Russia. The most visible security issues on which Ukraine had to contend with Russia concerned denuclearization and the division of the Black Sea Fleet. Even in this early period the basic characteristics of the Russian factor in relations between Ukraine and NATO were emerging. Although it was not often specifically mentioned, the role of this factor grew steadily and by the end of 1995 had become quite significant.

These developments were accompanied by the consolidation of the main lines of Russian foreign policy. However, Moscow's approach to NATO remained in flux. On the one hand, in June 1994 Moscow indicated its desire to cooperate with NATO by signing the PfP framework document, along with a special protocol which would grant Russia much more extensive rights and provisions than those obtained by the other partners of NATO. On the other hand, Russia expressed strong objection to NATO's enlargement plans; and later, on 14 September 1995, Boris Yeltsin issued a decree on the Strategic Policy of the Russian Federation towards CIS Member States, which foresaw action aimed at the restoration of Russian dominance over its CIS neighbours.

With Russia taking this kind of position, it took NATO a long time to reach agreement with Moscow on the Founding Act on Mutual Relations, Cooperation and Security between NATO and the Russian Federation, finally concluded in Paris on 27 May 1997. The Ukrainian authorities tend to believe that it was only after agreeing this Founding Act with Russia that NATO was ready to sign the Charter on a Distinctive Partnership between the North Atlantic Treaty Organization and Ukraine; in other words, that NATO's relations with Russia clearly influenced its policy towards Ukraine. This was the first substantial expression of the role of the Russian factor in relations between NATO and Ukraine. The former Ukrainian foreign minister suggests bitterly that 'of the two long years it took to make this idea a reality, 18 months were marked by a conspicuous lack of desire on the part of the Alliance to respond to our proposals. Only after a clear policy had been developed for attracting and involving Russia in NATO affairs was attention turned to Ukraine.'[2]

[2] B. Tarasiuk, 'Making the Ukraine–NATO Charter real. Opening remarks – Fulfilling the promise: building an enduring security partnership between Ukraine and NATO', in *The Stanford-Harvard Preventive Defense Project*, vol. 1, no. 3, Jan. 1999, p. 23.

The process of preparing and concluding the Ukrainian–Russian Treaty of Friendship, Cooperation and Partnership (eventually signed on 31 May 1997) was accompanied by speculation in Russia about what might better prevent Ukraine from hypothetically joining NATO in future: signing the treaty, which formally settles territorial differences between Russia and Ukraine, but allows the stationing of the Russian Black Sea Fleet in Crimea, or not signing the treaty, which might further ignite Ukrainian nationalism and drive Ukraine towards protection by NATO. The same arguments were rehearsed again during the treaty ratification process in the Russian Duma, delaying the ratification for more than a year.

Also in 1997, Sea Breeze, the US–Ukrainian naval exercise in the spirit of PfP held near the Ukrainian coast, provoked a strong reaction from Russia because of the presence of the Russian Black Sea Fleet in Crimea and the sentiments of ethnic Russians there. The Black Sea Fleet was initially invited by Ukraine to take part in the exercise, and attended early planning meetings, but the attitude of the Russian naval officers quickly changed, apparently as the result of political orders. The United States was termed an 'invader', and Russian propaganda tried to incite the local populace to oppose the exercise. The pro-Russian Crimean Communist Party, led by Leonid Grach, staged demonstrations and protests. Grach complained that 'Ukraine is subjecting itself to colonising at the hands of NATO, which is the main instrument of international capitalism centred in Washington.'[3] This

<hr>

[3] C. Caryl, 'NATO and Ukraine are getting cosy. And the Russians are not amused,' *US News online*, *http://www.usnews.com/usnews/issue/ 970915/15ukra.htm.*

reaction persuaded the US organizers to change their initial plans in order to make the exercise look less provocative. However, the inherent challenge to Ukrainian sovereignty in Crimea was clearly an attempt to demonstrate to Kiev the trouble Moscow could cause in the event of Ukraine–NATO relations becoming (in the Russian view) too close. Nevertheless, in late 1998, Ukraine's state programme of cooperation with NATO to 2001 was signed by presidential decree. The adverse reaction in Moscow was predictable as Ukraine signed this document irrespective of opinion in Russia.

Ukraine's independence of approach was shown again clearly in spring 1999 during the NATO operation in Kosovo, when Russia severed almost all contacts with the alliance, but Ukraine did not. The Ukrainian executive branch limited its reaction to 'regret', though Ukraine's parliament adopted a harsh resolution calling for a review of the country's national security policy.

Several other developments deserve attention in the context of the Russian factor. Soon after the NATO operation in Kosovo started on 26 March 1999, the Ukrainian foreign minister, Borys Tarasiuk, and defence minister, Olexander Kuzmuk, were the first high-level foreign officials to travel to Belgrade in an attempt to persuade Slobodan Milosevic to cooperate with NATO. But NATO, preoccupied with the task of obtaining Moscow's support, did not view this visit as meaningful. This response – or lack of it – gave rise to suggestions that 'Ukraine might be getting the impression that Russia's confrontational attitude paid more dividends than Ukraine's cooperative approach.'[4]

Ukraine–NATO relations were tested again when Russian troops rapidly deployed from their peacekeeping operations in Bosnia to occupy Slatina airfield in Kosovo at the end of the NATO air operation. When Russia asked permission to cross Ukrainian airspace to reinforce the airfield, this request at first was denied – an indication that Ukraine was on NATO's side in this tense stand-off. But under Russian pressure, given the prospect of confrontation with Russia without a guarantee of NATO military support (as well as other factors such as the pro-Russian sentiments of a significant part of the population), Ukraine backed off. It is open to speculation whether episodes like this reveal the reality of Ukraine's current relations with NATO in the Russian context, despite the frequent rhetoric about the strategic importance of cooperation between Ukraine and the alliance.

It should be acknowledged that in the 1990s Russia did try to overcome its negative imperial legacy, for example building cooperative mechanisms with both NATO and Ukraine. Russia joined NATO's PfP programme, signed the Founding Act and cooperated with NATO peacekeeping endeavours; and with Ukraine, it signed and ratified the Treaty of Friendship, Cooperation and Partnership, concluded agreements on the division of the Black Sea Fleet, and (reluctantly) agreed on the delimitation of the Russian–Ukrainian border (although it has still not agreed to demarcation).

[4] D. Karns, *NATO Relations with Ukraine: Prospects for Progress* (Tufts University, Fletcher School of Law and Diplomacy, Tufts, April 2000), p.16.

Nevertheless, even after the 11 September terrorist acts in the United States, a majority of Russian civilian and military officials continue to evince critical attitudes towards relations between NATO and Ukraine. To date, many instances of Russian cooperation with NATO and with Ukraine appear as forced, uncomfortable activity prompted by fear and distrust, rather than actions taken in a sincere pursuit of Russian national and common East–West interests. Russia will probably continue its attempts to achieve more unilateral influence on NATO policy, while interpreting Ukraine–NATO cooperation as threatening those attempts, and is unlikely to approve further *rapprochement* between Ukraine and NATO.

Recent military-political developments

Russia does not accept the argument that NATO is an alliance of peaceful democratic countries. Russian politicians across practically the entire political spectrum go to some lengths to point out at every opportunity the imperfect adherence of some NATO member states to 'democratic values' in respect of treatment of national minorities, civil–military relations, relations with neighbours and other issues. Nevertheless the question remains why, despite President Putin's shift towards cooperation with NATO in the anti-terrorist campaign, many in Russia (especially in the military) oppose NATO in general.

In the absence of real rather than hypothetical or perceived issues of conflict between Russia and NATO, the main reason for Russian opposition to NATO is in many cases probably an internal one – the survival of a post-imperial trauma, the wounded psyche of a former superpower, the difficulty many Russians find in openly admitting their country's weakness *vis-à-vis* NATO. Overcoming these psychological barriers will take some time and patience on NATO's part.

Still, the reality of the Russian position must impact on Russian calculations; Russia understands that it is comparatively weak and that NATO is strong, and that the only way to influence this unpleasant reality is to continue cooperative relations and try to promote its own agenda through these relations, rather than to close the door on cooperation. The first clear manifestations of this approach can be traced back to the spring of 2000, after the election of Vladimir Putin as Russian president. Soon thereafter, at the May 2000 EAPC foreign ministerial meeting in Florence, Russia returned to participation in the Euro-Atlantic Partnership Council. Subsequently, an 'ambitious' NATO–Russia Work Programme for 2001 was signed, marking the beginnings of a slow warming of the post-Kosovo chill in NATO–Russian relations.

In Ukraine this development was generally welcomed, as it was considered beneficial to Ukraine's own security.[5] But in Russia itself, suspicion of Ukraine's cooperation with the alliance remained deep and was regularly voiced. 'Do you understand what NATO's presence in Ukraine means? It means that an hour after the start of hostilities, the Northern Caucasus will be cut off,' the well-known Soviet-era dissident Alexander Solzhenitsyn predicted.[6]

[5] 'Readiness of Russia to soften its NATO stance is beneficial to Ukraine's security: expert opinion', Interfax-Ukraine, 11 May 2000.
[6] C. Kirillova, 'The patriarch and his adherents', *Stolichnye Novosti*, 23–29 May 2000.

Those sentiments were echoed by the Black Sea Fleet Commander Admiral Komoyedov in *Nezavisimaya Gazeta*: 'Such a "game" cannot but bother Russia ... to face Europe means turning one's back on Russia.'[7]

Some Russian politicians, in contrast, accept the utility of Ukraine and Russia moving jointly towards Europe. But many would not be averse to their neighbour remaining weak and indecisive. This partially explains the fact that so far Russian officials, unlike those of NATO, have never voiced their concern about the weakness of Ukraine's defence, or the slow pace of its military reform. By implication, Ukraine's problems in reconstructing its armed forces are more acceptable to Moscow than Ukraine's successes in that area.

The appointment by President Putin of the former Russian prime minister Victor Chernomyrdin as ambassador to Ukraine and presidential envoy with special responsibility for the development of Russian–Ukrainian trade and economic ties (without waiting for the formal endorsement of the Russian State Duma or the formal consent of the Ukrainian ministry of foreign affairs which is usually required) created a furore in Kiev. This reflected the fact that Chernomyrdin had been a prominent figure within the Russian natural gas industry – and that Ukraine's dependence upon Russian energy sources provides Moscow with its most powerful leverage. The additional title suggested that Chernomyrdin had

[7] Natalia Airapetova, 'Black Sea Fleet is ready to fulfill any mission (and its problems, according to the Fleet's commander Admiral Vladimir Komoedov, have their roots in Moscow)', *Nezavisimaya Gazeta*, 8 April 2000.

been tasked with exploiting such economic leverage; which could in turn be interpreted as evidence of Putin's intent to link Ukraine closer to Russia (and away from independent relations with NATO and the West in general) through upgraded economic ties.

However, the Ukrainians' positive attitude to the West does not depend solely on the fluctuations of the country's economic fortunes or the state of economic cooperation with Russia. A public opinion poll carried out by the Sociological Service of the Razumkov Centre in October 2001 indicated that among the different possible directions of Ukraine's foreign policy, 31% of its citizens prefer relations with EU countries as opposed to 26% who see relations with Russia as a priority (among the other choices were 'CIS countries without Russia', 'USA' and 'others').[8] If we compare the results of a similar public opinion poll a year earlier (June 2000), when 29% favoured EU countries and 26% favoured Russia, the conclusion could be drawn that, in general, the Western orientation in Ukraine is relatively strong and even growing. While the Ukrainian leadership has recently increased the number of friendly gestures made towards Russia, it has not terminated similar gestures towards NATO. In March 2001 the Ukrainian foreign ministry even dared to issue an official note protesting against the training of Russian Black Sea Fleet marines on the territory of a nature reserve in the Crimean mountains without prior coordination with Ukrainian authorities (the training was presented by the Russian TV channel RTR as preparation of servicemen for combat action in Chechnya).

[8] See *National Security and Defence*, no. 11, 2001.

Moreover, while Russians (especially officials in the foreign ministry, defence ministry and on the general staff) are still enamoured of the concept of 'zones of influence', it is reasonable to believe that the globalization of economics and information are trends beyond their control. Also, if Russia progresses further down the path of reform, there is no reason why Ukraine should not capitalize on good neighbourly economic relations with Russia. According to a recent Razumkov Centre public opinion poll, a clear majority of the Ukrainian population – 78.2% – see the economy as the major priority in Ukraine–Russia relations, as compared to only 23.3% who view security cooperation as the priority.[9]

After NATO's operation in Kosovo in 1999, Russia moved increasingly towards the periphery of the alliance's agenda. In this period, before 11 September, Russia was considered less in terms of a threat, or even an opponent, and the challenge of the relationship was represented in terms of managing Russia's weakness. This approach may account for the refusal of European NATO countries to seize the opportunity to engage Russia (and Ukraine) in the Western security system through joint participation in the development of the Antonov AN-7x military transport aircraft. The decision to reject the Ukrainian–Russian AN-7x project indicated that domestic policy and military–industrial interests were driving NATO politics much more strongly than security concerns.

In February 2001 Russia made another attempt to attract the attention of NATO by proposing the contribution of Russian technology and cooperation in the

[9] Ibid., p. 17.

creation of a European theatre missile defence (in which Ukraine could also play a role, given its capability to produce missiles and radar systems). The Russian liberal security analyst and prominent member of the State Duma Alexey Arbatov even suggested that this initiative could be regarded as something just short of a proposal of a security alliance by Russia with NATO.[10] However, this proposal was stillborn, although the question of missile defence is a subject for potential discussions in the new NATO–Russia Council established in spring 2002.

Recent military-technical developments

In the military-technical sphere Ukraine and Russia continue to be both partners in the production of weapons and competitors in the arms market. A close partnership between Ukraine and Russia was inherited from their common Soviet past, but Ukrainian independence brought to Moscow among other unpleasant consequences one more competitor in the arms trade. Despite Russian objections, Ukraine managed to produce and sell independently several weapons systems, which competed with the Russian niche, not the NATO one. In many areas Russia is unable to substitute for Ukrainian capabilities and expertise: Moscow depends, for example, on Ukrainian-produced homing warheads, various types of radar, and special targeting equipment for pilots' helmets. In 2001 Ukrainian space rockets performed four launches carrying Russian satellites.

[10] A. Arbatov, presentation to the Senior Executive Seminar, George C. Marshall European Center for Security Studies, Garmisch-Partenkirchen, Germany, 27 April 2001.

At the same time, Ukraine's major weapons systems are even more dependent on Russian supplies. Currently, due to the technological link and a currency shortage, Ukraine must buy spare parts and equipment for the Ukrainian armed forces almost exclusively from Russia. Partly as a result, Ukraine has more agreements in the military-technical sphere with Russia than with any other country – almost twenty in total.

It is hardly surprising in this sensitive situation that Russian officials have been opposed to cooperation between Ukraine (a Russian partner, client and minor competitor) and NATO (a perceived threat and major competitor). They suspect NATO countries of attempts to make Ukraine another client for their armaments to the detriment of Russian interests, and they also suspect Ukraine of possibly sharing sensitive information with NATO. For example, in an interview during the Abu Dhabi arms exhibition of 2001, the director-at-large of the Russian state weapons trade company Rosoboron-export, Colonel-General Nikolay Demidiuk, stated point blank that 'every step, however small, that takes Ukraine towards NATO is not only a matter of concern to Russia, but also cancels all preliminary agreements [in the area of military-technical cooperation]'.[11] His colleague expressed outrage that the Ukrainian deputy secretary of the National Security and Defence Council had tried to obtain information on Russian arms exports (which go through Ukrainian ports); he warned that such inform-ation would never be shared, and that attempts to gain

[11] V. Badrak, 'The era of intellectual weapons', *Dzerkalo Tyzhnia*, 24 March 2001.

access to it could possibly lead Russia to cancel its use of Ukrainian port facilities for arms shipments.[12]

However, it appears that to date Ukraine is not planning to curb its slowly growing arms trade and development projects with NATO countries in order to meet Russian concerns. It installed the Deutz German engine and the American Ariston gearbox into a new Ukrainian armoured personnel carrier, which it sells in turn to the United Arab Emirates. Ukraine already has a positive record of cooperation with France (with SAGEM and GIAT Industrie) in using French night vision equipment and fire control systems for Ukrainian tanks and other fighting vehicles. It sold two hovercraft ships of the Zubr type to Greece, and prospects for cooperation in the military-technical sphere with Greece and other European NATO countries are growing. In 2001 the Ukrainian border troops bought from Motorola more than 2,500 UHF radio stations – both mobile and stationary – and they intended to buy even more in 2002.

As an important step on this road, it is considered necessary to expedite the conclusion of agreements on the management of secret information. On 4 September 2001 such an agreement was signed with Poland.[13] Similar arrangements are pending with other NATO countries.

The new Ukrainian programme of cooperation with NATO devotes a special, apparently rather ambitious chapter to military-technical cooperation: chapter 6, on

[12] Ibid.

[13] 'In 2002 the process of Ukrainian units' participation in activities of Polish EU rapid reaction brigade will start', *Defense-Express*, 25 Oct. 2001, *http://www.defence-ua.com*.

'Cooperation in the sphere of armaments, standardization, defence research and technologies'. For Ukraine, the development of cooperation with NATO in the military-technical sphere is not in conflict with the development of cooperation with Russia, but represents an effort to achieve and maintain some sort of balance. Continuing Ukrainian overdependence on Russian military supplies will only strengthen Russia's control over Ukraine. Of course, Russia knows this, so one may expect continuing Russian political objections to Ukraine–NATO cooperation in the military-technical sector.

However, by the end of 2002 it was becoming increasingly evident to Russia that a restrictive approach towards military-technical cooperation with Ukraine is unproductive, acting only as a powerful incentive for Ukraine to seek cooperation with NATO. As a result, several agreements have recently been reached between Russia and Ukraine in areas such as the arms trade, joint air-to-air missiles and cooperation in the development and production of armoured vehicles, among others.

Ukraine and the new phase of NATO–Russia cooperation

The establishment of the new NATO–Russia Council provides a new opportunity to develop relations between NATO and Russia on the basis of firm cooperation, which in the long run can only benefit Ukraine–NATO relations. However, despite this new momentum for collaboration after the tragic events on 11 September 2001 in the United States, it is still very likely that in the short-term future Russian policies towards relations both with NATO and with Ukraine will remain a compromise between two approaches, one cooperative and the other disruptive.

Many in NATO and in Ukraine believe that the terrorist attack on the United States may result in positive changes in the relations between Russia and the United States/NATO. However, sceptics in both Russia and the West have pointed out possible impediments to a full-scale *rapprochement*. For instance, the alleged US 'preference for ad hoc relations unencumbered by the ponderous legal protocol of the past', in contrast to Russia's expectations 'to receive a seat at the Western table, one rooted in solid documentation', is regarded as a sign that 'the new partnership could easily founder upon a piece of paper – or the lack of one.'[14]

President Putin faces substantial, if not always open, opposition to aspects of this partnership with Western states in the anti-terrorist coalition. The traditional anti-American agenda is still alive and well in Russian politics and among Russian military elites. There is evidence that Russia's military and security officials have from the outset been particularly concerned about any American military presence in the former Soviet republics of central Asia north of Afghanistan – Uzbekistan, Kyrgyzstan and Tajikistan. Their concerns include the possibility of spying on Russian military facilities by American planes and the possible weakening of Russia's positions in those countries.[15]

[14] 'Russia remains skeptical of paperless disarmament', *Christian Science Monitor*, 4 Jan. 2002.
[15] A. Uzelac, 'Central Asia is crux of dilemma', *Moscow Times*, 21 Sept. 2001.

Similar sentiments are regularly expressed by Russian security officials and diplomats on the issue of NATO enlargement with regard to the possible candidacy of former Soviet republics,[16] above all, the three Baltic states and Ukraine. On 8 November 2001 the secretary of the Russian National Security Council, Vladimir Rushaylo, told reporters in Moscow that 'The pooling of international efforts to fight terrorism must not be used to justify the plans for NATO's eastward expansion.'[17] Whether by coincidence or not, Rushaylo's declaration was echoed in Kiev the same day by a high-level Russian diplomat, the acting *chargé d'affaires* in Ukraine, Aleksey Sazonov: 'Russia has a negative attitude to the process of NATO expansion to the East, it doesn't see valid reasons for that and doesn't understand justification voiced in support of that.'[18]

In general, it could be concluded that, at least in outward appearance, the official Russian policy towards NATO is becoming more sober and pragmatic, which gives some hope that in the future it may change towards recognition that there is no reasonable alternative to building truly cooperative relations with the alliance. However, in internal substance Russian foreign and security policy still remains opposed to Ukrainian–NATO cooperation, and will most probably continue thus at least for the next five to six years. It is unlikely

---

[16] See e.g. 'NATO, Russia maneuver as Baltics watch', *Chicago Tribune*, 3 Jan. 2002; V. Socor, 'Putin's "Near-abroad" gambit in the Baltics', *Wall Street Journal Europe*, 4 Jan. 2002.
[17] 'Fight against terrorism no reason to expand NATO, says Russian security chief', ITAR-TASS, Moscow, 8 Nov. 2001.
[18] 'Russia doesn't understand justification in favor of NATO expansion to the East', Interfax-Ukraine, 8 Nov. 2001.

that the Russian concern about the depth of cooperation between Ukraine and NATO will subside in the near future, or that Russia will abandon its effort to keep Ukraine in Russia's shadow. For example, an opinion poll of experts carried out in Russia in 2000 revealed that 84% of the Russian elite consider 'the deepening of Ukraine's cooperation with NATO' as the main negative factor in Russian–Ukrainian bilateral relations. In the light of such findings, it may take some time for the Russian elite to understand fully that NATO is not so much an enemy as a potential ally in Russia's 'real threat' environment.

3 UKRAINE'S PEACEKEEPING WITH NATO

Section III of the Charter on a Distinctive Partnership between the North Atlantic Treaty Organization and Ukraine, 'Areas for consultation and/or cooperation between NATO and Ukraine', specifies the importance of 'Ukrainian participation in operations, including peacekeeping operations'. Peacekeeping has indeed been prominent in this cooperation, and practical, visible achievements have been made. Although there are promising developments in Ukraine–NATO cooperation in other areas – defence reform, emergency assistance, scientific cooperation, the reintegration into civilian society of retired military personnel, etc., the scale of both effort and achievement in the field of peacekeeping, in terms of personnel, funds and time invested, and of gains in interoperability and practical experience, outweighs those in any other form of interaction.

Extracts from NATO–Ukraine official documents for the period 1996–2001 indicate the salience of the peacekeeping agenda:[1]

- NATO ministers welcomed Ukraine's continued support for SFOR and its recent decision to contribute an aircraft to the NATO air verification mission in Kosovo.

- NATO ambassadors highly appreciated Ukraine's contribution to the NATO-led peacekeeping operation

[1] See NATO website, *http://www.nato.int/docu/press.htm.*

in Bosnia–Herzegovina. They welcomed Ukraine's untiring efforts in the search for a peaceful settlement of the Kosovo crisis and looked forward to Ukrainian participation in an international civil and security presence in Kosovo.

- NATO ministers expressed their appreciation for the Ukrainian military contribution to IFOR and SFOR, and noted that Ukraine will focus its future troop contributions in the Balkans on KFOR.

- Ukraine and NATO confirmed their determination to continue their close cooperation within KFOR to restore security in Kosovo.

- NATO and Ukraine confirmed their determination to continue close cooperation within KFOR, and expressed their appreciation for its continuing crucial role in maintaining stability in Kosovo. Members of the Commission[2] gave a positive assessment of Ukraine's practical contribution to KFOR through its helicopter unit and the contribution to the Polish–Ukrainian peacekeeping battalion.[3]

Ukraine's contribution to NATO peacekeeping

Ukrainians were always regarded as good soldiers and good fighters. As early as 1992, soon after becoming independent, Ukraine began its participation in UN

[2] The NATO–Ukraine Commission established by the 1997 charter.
[3] The Polish–Ukrainian battalion is a joint peacekeeping formation that was set up in 1997 and became operational in 2000. It is organized into joint battalion headquarters, four companies (two from each country) and support elements. Its current total strength is almost 700 (327 Ukrainian and 367 Polish military personnel).

peacekeeping operations.[4] By the middle of 2002 there were almost 1,700 Ukrainian peacekeepers carrying out responsibilities in ten peacekeeping operations around the globe. Since 1992, almost 20,000 Ukrainians have been engaged in peacekeeping missions; twenty-six have lost their lives and more than fifty have been wounded.

Ukraine also has a strong record of peacekeeping cooperation with NATO. Between 1995 and 1999 some 2,800 Ukrainian peacekeepers fulfilled peacekeeping duties in the IFOR and SFOR missions in Bosnia-Herzegovina, serving either in the 400-strong Ukrainian 240th Special Mechanized Battalion or in staff elements of IFOR and SFOR. Each year during the period 1996–9 Ukraine's government authorized expenditure of some $6–7 million to cover the expenses of Ukrainian peace-keepers in the former Yugoslavia.

From the summer of 1999 to the middle of 2002, over 2,500 Ukrainians were engaged in peacekeeping activities in cooperation with NATO in Kosovo. Ukraine has contributed to KFOR the Ukrainian element of the joint Polish–Ukrainian battalion, which in July 2000 replaced the Ukrainian 37th Detached Mechanized Company, and the 14th Helicopter Squadron. The heli-copter squadron, which returned to Ukraine in the spring of 2001, comprised 63 personnel and four Mi-8 helicop-ters; it has flown 6,500 missions in direct support of COMKFOR, transporting over 200 tonnes of equipment and over 20,000 personnel, including MEDEVAC and

[4] On 3 July 1992 the Verkhovna Rada (parliament) of Ukraine adopted a resolution 'On participation of the battalions of the armed forces of Ukraine in the UN peacekeeping forces in conflict zones on the territory of former Yugoslavia'.

VIP transport. The crews displayed excellent operational skills and had an outstanding record of flight safety in a challenging environment. This contribution was important to KFOR overall at a time when the force's helicopter assets were stretched.

The Ukrainian element (currently numbering 327 individuals) of the Polish–Ukrainian Battalion (UKRPOLBAT or POLUKRBAT), located in Camp White Eagle near the village of Raka, remains in Kosovo and provides security in the Multinational Brigade East (MNB E). The tasks of the Ukrainian contingent of the MNB are as follows:

- to monitor, verify and enforce as necessary the provisions of the Military Technical Agreement in order to secure a safe and secure environment;

- to provide humanitarian assistance in support of the UNHCR efforts;

- to enforce basic law and order;

- to establish and support the resumption of core civil functions;

- to conduct checkpoints, observation posts, patrolling and convoy operations in AOR.

In November 2000 Ukrainian personnel were involved in the seizure of a large arms cache. Since March 2001 Ukrainians have been involved in KFOR operations along the border with the Former Yugoslav Republic of Macedonia near Mijak. During September–October 2001 UKRPOLBAT participated in the operation 'Border and Search' on twelve occasions. The successful execution of these and other missions contributed to a broader common evaluation by NATO and Ukraine of peace-keeping tasks in the Balkans. NATO Secretary-General George Robertson was unequivocal in May 2001: 'NATO and Ukraine continue to see eye to eye in the Balkans. Our joint work in Kosovo demonstrates that our partnership is not just a fair-weather affair … Jointly we remain committed to a stable Balkan region and to other issues of regional security'.[5]

This assessment reflects the whole range of Ukraine–NATO activities within the partnership working programme, including regular training exercises under and 'in the spirit of' PfP, a variety of courses, military visits, etc. Since 1997 Ukraine's participation in the planning and review process (PARP) within PfP has become increasingly active. In the first place, PARP is supposed to enhance the interoperability of Ukrainian units participating in PfP activities with NATO forces according to NATO standards. But from 2001 the focus of PARP has been widened in order to help Ukraine to achieve some of its goals for overall defence reform. These objectives are facilitated by the experience accumulated by the personnel of the Department for Military Cooperation and Verification within the general staff of the armed forces of Ukraine, where cooperation with NATO and peacekeeping issues are currently guided by the deputy chief of the department, Major General Leonid Holopatiuk. This work is carried out together with the NATO liaison office in Ukraine, currently headed by Captain Leigh Merrick (RN, retd.).

[5] Opening statement by NATO Secretary-General Lord Robertson at the meeting of the NATO–Ukraine Commission at foreign minister level, Budapest, 30 May 2001.

Cooperation between NATO and Ukraine towards closer interoperability enabled the two sides to plan an unprecedented PfP tactical exercise in 2002, named Cooperative Adventure Exchange. The plan envisioned the participation of 5,000 troops in an exercise to be held at the Yavoriv peacekeeping training centre in October 2002.

Lessons learned from the experience of Ukraine in NATO peacekeeping

Overall, certain lessons can be learned from the experience of Ukraine in NATO peacekeeping operations.

First, participation in joint peacekeeping operations lays a solid foundation for possible future participation in joint operations, whether for peacekeeping or combat purposes. However, doctrine (and training in that doctrine) is a more important 'glue' to hold different types of forces together than just bringing them both to the same level of interoperability in material–technical terms. In this regard, NATO efforts to build a 'hierarchy' of allied joint doctrine are important.

As regards interoperability, the joint execution of missions reveals the problems encountered by each contingent, as well as their individual strengths. The problems faced by Ukrainian troops include insufficient language training, deficiencies in manning levels and the equipping of the contingent.[6] However, the military

---

[6] See e.g. *Defense-Express*, 29 Dec. 2001: 'Defense-Express has reported that despite wide peacekeeping experience, the former peace-keepers are not effectively used as training instructors. Sources in the General Staff of the Armed Forces of Ukraine told Defense-Express that the

proficiency displayed by Ukrainian officers enabled them to work in the headquarters of the KFOR Multinational Brigade East. Both Polish and Ukrainian officers from UKRPOLBAT headquarters were invited by the US military to participate in the certification of the US 1st Infantry Division in Germany.[7]

The second important lesson of Ukraine's peacekeeping with NATO for future joint peacekeeping operations is that multinational peacekeeping formations contribute to the more effective accomplishment of missions through increased understanding and interoperability between NATO member countries and NATO partners. Ukrainian and Polish experience has proved that such units are not just an exercise in high-profile political demonstrations of bilateral and multilateral cooperation, but could be a practical tool – a force multiplier.

The experience of the joint Polish–Ukrainian peacekeeping battalion may have contributed to the establishment of other units, for example the Tisa multinational engineers battalion, which combines units from Ukraine with units from Hungary, Romania and Slovakia. This initiative was suggested by Ukraine in December 1998; in January 1999 a protocol of understanding was signed on the creation of the formation; and in December 2001

---

selection of candidates for participation in peace-keeping missions is still imperfect, the proper database as well as the fact that the set of requirements which the AFU officers should meet to occupy the vacancies in multinational peace-keeping staffs has not yet been created. As a result, the selection procedures are often run subjectively.' See *http://www.defence-ua.com/eng/news/*.
[7] V. Voroniuk, 'Whom will General David go to fight with?', *Narodna Armiya*, 4 Jan. 2002.

the defence ministers of Ukraine, Romania and Slovakia signed a treaty in Brussels on the creation of the multinational engineers battalion. Hungary was not formally represented, as the country needed to amend some of its legal provisions to enable the participation of its military units in search and rescue operations. Ukraine and Romania will form two companies for the battalion, Slovakia and Hungary one company each. The Ukrainian element of the battalion (179 men and more than sixty items of engineering equipment) has already been organized. In May 2002 the first command post exercise of the joint battalion was held in Ukraine.

The experiences of and requirements for peacekeeping are taken into account by the Ukrainian Centre for Peacekeeping Activity and Cooperation with NATO, as well as by military training centres. Examinations in these requirements are held in Ukraine's National Academy of Defence, the Yavoriv PfP training centre and training centres of the individual services of Ukraine's armed forces, all of which receive support from NATO. The favourable assessment by NATO of the Yavoriv PfP training centre in particular is reflected in a NATO press release: 'The designation of the Yavoriv Training Area as a PfP training centre provides a useful instrument for joint exercises and training opportunities and we encourage all Partners to take advantage of them.'[8]

Of particular importance are courses for the officers of multinational staffs (currently headed and run by the former Ukrainian senior military representative in NATO headquarters, Lieutenant-General Vitaliy Kuksenko).

[8] See NATO press release NUC-S(99)68, 24 April 1999.

These train officers who are selected for positions in international peacekeeping or similar multinational staffs. For each two-week rotation up to forty officers study the theoretical foundations of peacekeeping, as well as practical Ukrainian and international experience in working on a multinational basis. The curriculum is based on programmes from NATO schools. Many of the course instructors come from outside Ukraine, from NATO and partner countries.

There is a plan to transform the courses for the officers of multinational staffs into a centre for training officers for peace support operations,[9] with the help of NATO. The special working group developing regulations on the preparation of peacekeeping units and personnel also works in cooperation with NATO.

In general, Ukraine–NATO cooperation on peacekeeping is progressively improving and broadening. It has reached the stage when NATO is considering cooperation with Ukraine in military operations beyond traditional peacekeeping. In autumn 2001 Ukraine, for its part, declared for the first time that the budget for international activities of the Ukrainian ministry of defence includes a specific line for expenditure in support of cooperation with NATO.[10]

[9] 'It is a difficult assignment – to build peace', *Narodna Armiya*, 27 Sept. 2001.
[10] See *Defense-Express*, 22 Dec. 2001: 'The provided expenditures for international activities of the military department are sufficiently supported – deputy minister of defense', *http://www.defence-ua.com/ eng/news/?id=1440*.

4 UKRAINE–NATO PEACEKEEPING IN THE BROADER CONTEXT

Ukraine and the EU: capitalizing on peacekeeping with NATO?

For more than half a century NATO, as a military-political alliance, has been at the core of west European defence; today, it remains the only workable defence structure in Europe. At the same time, given the existing differences in the interests of the allies, limitations caused by the military profile of NATO activity (with the principle of collective defence still at the heart of it) and the will of the Europeans to assume greater responsibility for their own security, pressures have mounted to develop an effective European security and defence structure. Such a structure is being actively developed under the auspices of the EU within the framework of the European Security and Defence Policy (ESDP).

For Ukraine, which has proclaimed accession to the EU as a strategic goal, the development of the ESDP offers the possibility of strengthening its distinctive partnership with NATO and at the same time developing security and defence relations with the EU. There appears to be a good mutual understanding between Ukraine and NATO on this subject, as expressed in the following statement in spring 2001:

> Ukraine welcomed NATO's continuing efforts to meet the changing circumstances in European security and

its role, together with other international organizations, such as the EU and the OSCE [Organization for Security and Cooperation in Europe], in promoting Euro-Atlantic security. In this context, NATO Allies, proceeding from the Charter on a Distinctive Partnership, welcomed Ukraine's initiative to consult on developments in the NATO–EU dialogue on the issues which have direct impact on the national security interests of Ukraine.[1]

Relations between NATO and the EU in the security domain are entering a decisive phase. At present, there is only one workable military-political structure in the European security system – NATO – and it is primarily based on the continued readiness of the United States to invest lavishly in the defence sector and maintain close ties with Europe. The EU remains dependent on the United States in the security sphere. It has claims to greater independence in that domain, but its readiness to back declarations of intent with substantial resources is still questionable.[2]

However, irrespective of the present uncertainty and contradictions in NATO–EU relations, Ukraine should develop ties with both institutions more actively. As an integral part of Europe, Ukraine is obliged to do this.

[1] Statement at meeting of the NATO–Ukraine Commission in ambassadorial session, press release (2001) 057, 4 May 2001.
[2] In numerical strength, the European component of NATO forces is more than twice that of the United States, but the military expenditures of the Europeans make up a meagre 64% of the US level. According to various assessments, the aggregate combat potential of the European NATO members amounts to between 10% and 30% of the potential of the United States, since the Europeans spend far less than the United States on research and development and weapons procurement.

For Ukraine, special relations with NATO are a precondition for deepening interaction with the alliance member countries and approaching its goal of EU membership. Ukraine can use its relations of partnership with NATO to participate in the development of the new system of European security, in particular through its contribution to joint peacekeeping efforts. Ukraine is ready for active cooperation with both NATO and the EU: it maintains relations of distinctive partnership with the alliance and is seeking to develop relations of strategic partnership with the EU. As Ukraine's foreign minister Anatoly Zlenko put it: 'Doctrinally, Ukraine shares the concept of the new Europe based on the European Union, the Council of Europe and the North Atlantic Treaty Organization. Exactly those institutions present the basic pillars of Ukraine's European course.'[3]

Cooperation between Ukraine and the EU in the sphere of foreign and security policy became a subject of discussion after the Ukraine–EU Partnership and Cooperation Agreement (PCA) came into effect in 1998.[4] Once the EU joint strategy towards Ukraine was adopted in 1999, the issue of institutionalizing relations between the two parties in the fields of foreign policy, security, military and military–technical cooperation came to the fore. In September 2000 Ukraine presented a memorandum on this topic to the EU.[5] The document was not

[3] A. Zlenko, speech delivered at the NATO–Ukraine symposium, 'The world in the 21st century: cooperation, partnership, dialogue', *Nauka i Oborona*, no. 3, 2001, p. 5.
[4] The agreement was signed and ratified in 1994 and became effective on 1 March 1998.
[5] V. Belashov, 'Revolution in European military affairs', *Polityka i Chas*, no. 5, 2001, p. 34.

made public, but apparently contained quite far-reaching proposals, which the EU was not ready to accept at that time.[6] In the same month, at the Ukraine–EU summit in Paris, various issues of cooperation in the field of CFSP were addressed separately. After that, political dialogue in the sector intensified significantly.[7]

In a joint statement after a Ukraine–EU summit held in Yalta in September 2001, the parties 'marked further progress of our dialogue, cooperation and consultations on security and defence issues' and noted that 'Ukraine may be invited to take part in operations conducted by the EU.'[8] Judging by the content of the core tasks in the area of EU security and defence policy – the 'Petersberg Tasks'[9] – it is not unreasonable to assume that Ukraine 'may be invited to take part' specifically in peacekeeping operations.

[6] In particular, the Ukrainian side proposed raising relations between Ukraine and the EU in the sphere of foreign and security policy to the level of 'distinctive or associated strategic partnership, following the example of relations with NATO, and made concrete proposals as to the mechanism of such partnership': ibid.
[7] During 2001, President Leonid Kuchma met the secretary-general of the European Council, the EU high representative for the Common Foreign and Security Policy, Javier Solana, four times.
[8] Recently, Ukraine again offered the EU its military transport aviation for ESDP purposes (in 1997 a document on 'Cooperation between Ukraine and WEU in the field of long-distance air transportation' was signed) and its military assets. It announced its intention to second a group of officers led by a general to the EU military staff; to contribute a strengthened air mobile battalion, a combined (transport and combat) helicopter squadron, a squadron of IL-76 aircraft from the air transport command of Ukraine's air force and some other military assets to the EU rapid reaction corps; and to provide the EU with nearly 500 policemen.
[9] At their meeting in Petersberg near Bonn in June 1992, the foreign and defence ministers of the Western European Union outlined the

There are already consultations in place on the scope of a possible Ukrainian contribution to EU peacekeeping and crisis response capabilities.[10] Top-level meetings have resulted in preliminary agreements on the possible assignment of a Ukrainian general as a permanent representative to EU command structures and the incorporation of a Ukrainian national component into the EU multinational rapid reaction brigade.

The structure of the multinational brigade has not yet been finally determined. It is expected to include a brigade headquarters; three to four national infantry (rifle, mechanized infantry, air-mobile) battalions; an artillery battalion; an anti-tank battalion (battery); an anti-aircraft artillery battalion; a reconnaissance company; a signal company; a field-engineer company; and logistic and maintenance units. It is also planned to employ a military police unit, an aviation reconnaissance and rescue squadron, and three navy ships to support the activities of the latter. Ukraine has offered to transfer five to ten officers to the joint headquarters of the multinational European rapid reaction brigade, as well as offering an air-mobile battalion and a combined aviation squadron.

---

range of CFSP tasks (the so-called 'Petersberg Tasks') – humanitarian and rescue tasks, peacekeeping tasks, tasks of combat forces in crisis management, including peacemaking – and coordinated the issues associated with putting assets and capabilities at the disposal of the EU.
[10] See e.g. Interfax-Ukraine, 28 July 2001: 'Kyiv and Warsaw negotiate the participation of a Ukrainian unit in a Polish brigade of the European security force. Jeshuv, Poland, 28 July 2001. Former Minister of Defence of Ukraine Olexander Kuzmuk believes that the inclusion of a Ukrainian unit in the Polish brigade will be a logical step to extend Polish–Ukrainian cooperation in the military field.'

Apart from its contribution to a multinational brigade, Ukraine can offer the EU an air transport squadron from its own air force for strategic airlift capability. A helicopter squadron and an air transport squadron are already participating in the third cycle of the NATO PARP process as part of the PfP programme. Another Ukrainian formation that may be employed in the interests of pan-European security is the multinational engineers battalion Tisa, mentioned in chapter 3. Ukraine has proposed using the Yavoriv peacekeeping training centre to train forces through field and command post exercises. Within the framework of Ukraine's participation in civilian aspects of crisis management under EU auspices, the provision of a detachment of police forces, as well as personnel and facilities for civil administration and protection of the population, is also possible.[11]

It is important to note that the population of Ukraine, according to an opinion poll conducted by the Razumkov Centre, has a generally favourable view of ESDP peacekeeping activity. The question whether Ukraine should 'directly participate in forming rapid reaction forces and peacekeeping operations under the EU auspices' was answered positively by nearly half of the respondents (49.7%) and negatively by 23.6%; 26.7% abstained. The majority of Ukrainians (57.3%) believe that the EU member states are interested in involving Ukraine in security and defence cooperation.[12]

[11] For more details, see 'Round table by correspondence', *National Security and Defence*, no. 9, 2001.
[12] For more details, see M. Pashkov, 'Problems of European security: positions of the population of Ukraine', *National Security and Defence*, no. 9, 2001.

However, to date real bilateral cooperation in the sphere of ESDP lags significantly behind the declared goals. The programme of Ukraine's integration into the EU defines the participation of Ukraine in the EU Common Foreign and Security Policy as a long-term priority (2004–7); it also states that 'at the present stage, Ukraine–EU relations in the security domain are at the stage of formation'. Section 17 of the programme, devoted to Ukraine's cooperation with the EU over issues of foreign and security policy, does not outline the financial requirements and other resources necessary for such cooperation, nor does it specify the sources of such funds.

Although the institutional level of Ukraine's cooperation with the EU in the security sphere lags behind the country's cooperation with NATO, concrete practical steps are being made in some directions. This is true primarily in the fields of justice and internal affairs, and has special significance in the context of EU enlargement: the EU is concerned with strengthening the security of its eastern borders after the accession of candidates from central Europe. The joint statement of the results of the Yalta Ukraine–EU summit stressed the 'common desire of the EU and Ukraine to fight organised crime, money laundering, illegal drug and arms trafficking, and closely cooperate in the issues of illegal immigration, refugees, smuggling and human trafficking'.

At present, assistance for the strengthening of borders is being granted not only to candidates for EU membership (Poland, Slovakia, Hungary), but also to Ukraine. In particular, significant financial assistance for strengthening the Ukraine–Russian border (DM 3 million in

2001) was extended by the German ministry of internal affairs, which enabled the protection of that border sector to be improved by the transfer of 60 units of border guards from the western border of Ukraine.[13] It is noteworthy that the flow of illegal migrants via Ukraine has significantly decreased – the annual total captured by Ukrainian border guards has fallen from more than 18,000 in the late 1990s, to about a third of that by 2000–2.

Within the framework of the Tacis programme, a separate project of technical assistance is being developed to strengthen Ukraine's state border with the Republic of Moldova and decrease the flow of illegal migrants on that segment; the European Commission has granted €3.9 million for that project. The EU also granted significant technical assistance in 2001 for the creation of the Narkobiznes interdepartmental databank in Ukraine, intended to raise the efficiency of combating illegal drug trafficking.

All in all, the experience of cooperation with the EU proves that Ukraine has realistic prospects of becoming a member of a united Europe at some stage in the future. The country can already contribute to European security in general and EU peacekeeping efforts in particular. To

[13] According to the first deputy commander of Ukraine's border troops, General-Colonel Pavlo Shisholin, 'now [Ukraine's] State Border Committee negotiates with German colleagues the issue of receiving the means of communication, monitoring, radar stations, infra-red field-glasses, high-speed military jeeps for use on the Byelorussian and Moldovan portions of the border.' See *Defense-Express*, 5 Jan. 2002, 'Presentation of the border troops program on granting the EU's help for arrangement of the Ukrainian Border will be held Jan. 30 in Brussels', *http://www.defence-ua.com*.

be sure, the speed of Ukraine's engagement with the EU will first and foremost depend on the strengthening of the democratic fundamentals of Ukraine's society and the development of the market economy. Despite the problems which exist in those areas, even in the present conditions, the potential for deepening Ukraine's cooperation with the EU in the security sphere should not be underestimated. Among other EU applicants Ukraine has a distinct position in the security domain; it is likely to be not only a consumer but a real contributor – in strategic transport, space, intelligence, peacekeeping, law enforcement, responding to natural and techno-logical disasters, etc.

Moreover, as observed previously, Ukraine may move towards membership of the EU both through direct cooperation with the Union and through using the channels available for cooperation with NATO: 'The status of Ukraine as a state that has distinctive relations with NATO opens real prospects to approach the start line where it could be seen as a potential member of the European Union.'[14]

So, what place can Ukraine occupy in the future Euro-pean security architecture? On whom does this depend – on the country itself, on the EU countries, or on the United States and NATO? Ultimately, Ukraine's future role will be conditioned by all these actors, but Ukraine is determined that its contribution and significant potential in peacekeeping should not be forgotten.

[14] V. Horbulin, speech delivered at the NATO–Ukraine symposium, 'The world in the 21st century: cooperation, partnership, dialogue', *Nauka i Oborona*, no. 3, 2001, p. 9.

Peacekeeping in GUUAM: a frozen potential to be thawed by NATO?

Ukraine has also tried to develop a southern axis of strategic partnership, with the GUUAM (Georgia, Ukraine, Uzbekistan, Azerbaijan and Moldova) group.

Multilateral cooperation among the member states of this group commenced in 1996, in Vienna, during the negotiations on the Conventional Forces in Europe (CFE) Treaty, at which the delegations of Azerbaijan, Georgia, Moldova and Ukraine for the first time provided joint statements and initiatives.[15] At the initial stage, in particular, in the course of negotiations about a multilateral agreement on flank limitations in Europe,[16] the *rapprochement* between Azerbaijan, Georgia, Moldova and Ukraine (GUAM) was based largely on a desire to pool their efforts in search of new arguments in their dialogue with Russia. At the same time, the idea of a new southern arc of states characterized by a common approach to the formation of the strategic transport corridor from Europe through the Caucasus to Asia was conducive to further regional integration.

A system of consultative contacts at various levels gradually developed.[17] The format of a political–consultative

[15] For a detailed analysis of the state and prospects of major GUUAM areas of cooperation, see *National Security and Defence*, no. 7, 2001. Uzbekistan left the group in 2002, and its acronym has now reverted to GUAM.
[16] Limitations on the deployment of heavy armaments in certain areas, in accordance with the Flank Documents of 1996.
[17] Political consultations at the level of deputy foreign ministers were held in Baku on 25 November 1997. Foreign ministers of the GUAM member states met in Copenhagen on 18 December 1997 and in Oslo on 2 December 1998. Heads of delegations from Ukraine,

forum enabled the formulation of common positions in the UN and OSCE as well as coordinated decisions on international issues.[18] On 24 April 1999, at the Washington NATO summit, Uzbekistan joined GUAM, and the presidents of the five countries made a declaration outlining the basic directions of cooperation of what was now called GUUAM: in essence, strengthening all forms of cooperation at international organizations and forums, and pursuing greater interaction within the EAPC and the NATO PfP programme. The summit, held in a period of sharp deterioration in NATO–Russian relations, demonstrated the intention of the GUUAM member states to dissociate themselves from Russia and intensify cooperation with the North Atlantic alliance.

At the Yalta GUUAM summit held on 6–7 June 2001, the presidents of the member states signed the Yalta Charter of GUUAM – a statutory document that specified the goals, principles, lines of cooperation and organizational structure of the group. It defined the annual meeting of the heads of states as the supreme body of GUUAM, meetings of the ministers of foreign affairs as the executive body, and the Committee of National Coordinators as its working body.

It is noteworthy that, in contrast to preliminary documents for the summit, and numerous previous steps towards developing a peacekeeping component within GUUAM, the charter makes no mention of joint

Georgia, Moldova and Azerbaijan met in October 1998, during the annual IMF session in Washington.

[18] For instance, decisions of the Istanbul OSCE summit (1999) on withdrawal of Russian troops from territories of the GUUAM member states.

peacekeeping activities, assistance in the management of regional conflicts or the intensification of relations with Euro-Atlantic structures, which were all present in earlier documents of the group.[19] Independent observers attributed this to heavy pressure from Russia.

It is interesting to note that neither experts nor the population at large in Ukraine had any illusion about the feasibility at this stage of GUUAM developing into anything resembling a military alliance. According to a sociological study conducted by Razumkov Centre in spring 2001, half of the experts (50%) were inclined to believe that GUUAM is a group of countries united to counteract Russian influence in the post-Soviet space. Among Ukrainian citizens the opinion was quite different – only one out of six interviewed (16.1%) supported this view. A considerably smaller number of experts (36%) were convinced that GUUAM is a consultative group of countries set up to resolve jointly specific international issues. This view was supported by one-fifth of the population (20.9%). Only 4% of both experts and the population were of the opinion that GUUAM is a military-political bloc aiming at enhancing contacts with NATO. In other words, so far both the general population and the Ukrainian establishment see GUUAM as a regional business project rather than any kind of military-political alliance.[20]

[19] The charter provides for cooperation in the following areas: 'Economy, science, technology and environment; infrastructure of transport, energy, telecommunications; joint investment and financial projects; the humanitarian sector, culture, education, mass media, tourism, youth exchanges; other domains of mutual interest'.
[20] V. Chaly and M. Pashkov, 'GUUAM as assessed by the elite and the population of Ukraine', *Dzerkalo Tyzhnia*, 2 June 2001.

However, for Ukraine, participation in GUUAM makes sense only if it promotes the international positions of the state, its economic development and regional security. Consequently, the idea of reviving efforts to develop peacekeeping activities within the framework of GUUAM has not been permanently sidelined.[21] As mentioned above, the member states originally initiated cooperation in the format of GUAM in the military sphere, when issues relating to the limits on CFE in Europe were being negotiated. Later, attempts were made to establish military cooperation among the member states, and joint military activities were organized. However, at the June 2001 Yalta summit the institutionalization of the military and peacekeeping component of GUUAM did not occur; leaders of the member states formally denied the very possibility of transforming the union into a military-political alliance, and refrained from any reference to GUUAM or joint military-technical projects. Nevertheless, preconditions for deepening cooperation among the member states in the military sphere (particularly in peacekeeping) do exist.

The prospects for cooperation in the security domain are not confined to purely military aspects.[22] All the

[21] This possibility may be suggested by information about a meeting between GUUAM countries' representatives and their counterparts from the United States to discuss security issues. See 'Representatives of GUUAM countries and the USA discuss in Baku the issues of transport corridors' security', Interfax-Ukraine, 7 Nov. 2001. The agency cites several senior officials speaking about cooperation on issues of border security, security of the transport corridors, fighting international crime, drug trafficking, etc. Following the meeting further consultations between GUUAM and the United States are envisioned.
[22] The importance of military and other aspects of security cooperation was stressed by the former foreign minister of Ukraine,

GUUAM countries are more or less threatened by terrorism, drug trafficking, international crime, separatism, and natural and man-made disasters. Exactly those aspects of security were reflected in the Yalta 2001 GUUAM Charter.

Cooperation of the GUUAM member states in the military sphere is conditioned by many common traits: the common Soviet military heritage (weapons systems, regulatory base, operational procedures, field manuals, even the military's post-Soviet evolutions); the defensive character of their military doctrines; adherence to international arms control and disarmament regimes; attempts to participate in peacekeeping activities;[23] and active participation in the NATO PfP programme. The member states are taking measures to reform their armed forces and revive production at defence enterprises; and they are seeking to introduce civilian control over the defence sector. Another common feature of the GUUAM member states is the existence of open or latent internal conflicts on their territories.

The mutual commitments of the GUUAM member states in the military sphere do not provide for military assistance in the event of a threat to the sovereignty or territorial integrity of any of the member states. In the event of a threat of aggression, therefore, Ukraine cannot

---

Borys Tarasiuk, in his article 'GUUAM: the sources and prospects', *National Security and Defence*, no. 7, 2001.

[23] Ukraine has been taking an active part in peacekeeping operations since 1992, but the activity of other GUUAM member states in that sphere remains limited: Azerbaijan and Georgia sent one peacekeeper platoon each to Kosovo, and Uzbekistan was a participant in the former collective CIS peacekeeping forces in Tajikistan.

count on military support from its GUUAM partners. This conclusion is reinforced by the condition of the armed forces of the GUUAM member states and the results of a Razumkov Centre expert poll. The armed forces of the member states have a limited military potential and lack a significant mobile component. If a military-political alliance were established within the framework of GUUAM, Ukraine would assume the main burden, since its military potential exceeds the aggregate capabilities of the other member states.

Poll results show that the overwhelming majority (81%) of the experts polled do not believe in the ability of GUUAM partners to render military support to Ukraine in the event of a threat. Razumkov Centre sociological surveys show that Ukrainian experts are rather sceptical about GUUAM's military potential, compared to other post-Soviet regional unions: only 8% of experts consider it to be high, and 29% put it at average. Public opinion is very much the same: 8.3% and 15.3% of those polled, respectively.[24]

It is clear, therefore, why the member states avoid describing GUUAM as a structure aiming to establish a new military-political alliance within the CIS. Even before Uzbekistan joined GUAM, the Georgian president Eduard Shevardnadze had said that the group 'is not a union, moreover not a military bloc, and poses no threat to the CIS whatsoever'. According to his words, GUAM was created solely for the coordination of the positions

[24] One should take into account that awareness of the GUUAM problems among the population is not high: nearly half of all respondents made no assessment of the military potential of GUUAM and other post-Soviet unions.

of the member states on the issue of conventional arms reduction in Europe.[25]

There are a number of additional impediments to any aspirations to peacekeeping in a GUUAM format: the scarcity of funds of the member states for this purpose; the need to obtain a UN or OSCE mandate (for participation in a UN peacekeeping operation, the requirement for impartiality of the participants must be met, which would be difficult in the case of GUUAM); and the influence of key international actors. Furthermore, GUUAM might obtain the formal right to conduct independent peacekeeping operations only after it is transformed into a fully-fledged regional organization.

Analysis of the military-political interaction among the GUUAM member states suggests that in the medium term the grouping is unlikely to be transformed into a military-political alliance, both for geopolitical reasons and because of the limited capabilities of its members. If large-scale joint economic, energy and transport projects were to be implemented and a military threat were to emerge, the issue of the defence of joint interests would arise. But the format and scale of military-political cooperation in this case would probably be determined not by the GUUAM member states alone, but by all the participants in the respective projects and other countries of the region.

In 1998–9, attempts were made to establish multilateral military cooperation within GUUAM. The climax of those efforts was the attempt to form a joint peacekeeping battalion of GUUAM. However, both that and

[25] See Interfax-Ukraine, 10 March 1999.

other attempts at reviving multilateral military cooperation within GUUAM failed. 'Multilateral' cooperation among the member states took place only within the framework of the existing and quite effective NATO format – the PfP programme.

The spirit and directions of military cooperation within GUUAM were determined by regular meetings of the defence ministers of the member states. In January 1999, after several attempts, they met in Baku and resolved that

> military cooperation in the framework of GUAM is called to play an important role in the establishment of a reliable system of providing security in the region, while defence departments should more closely co-operate on the issues of raising the defence capability of the armies, the settlement of conflicts and the performance of peacekeeping missions.

At the next meeting in March 1999 in Tbilisi, which included the defence ministers of Azerbaijan, Georgia and Ukraine, a protocol was signed on a joint exercise to be held on the Yalgudszha range in Georgia.

Later, however, interest in such joint meetings faded, and this was particularly clear in 2000–1. A meeting of defence ministers planned for January 2000 in Georgia never occurred; and an attempt to hold such a meeting during the 2000 CIS summit in Moscow also failed. To fill the gap in contacts, in March 2000 the deputy chiefs of staff of the GUUAM member states met in Kiev (without the Uzbek representative). The heads of the GUUAM defence ministries gave preference to bilateral meetings – for example, in October 2000 the Ukrainian defence minister paid a visit to Uzbekistan, and the

Azerbaijani minister visited Kiev; the Georgian minister of defence came to Ukraine on an official visit in February 2001. In recent years, Ukraine has implemented relatively small annual plans of bilateral military cooperation (some five to ten events per year) with the GUUAM countries. This orientation towards bilateral cooperation is supported by the Ukrainian foreign ministry.[26]

One possible way of reviving military cooperation among the GUUAM member states was the formation of a joint unit that could take part in maintaining the security of the oil transport corridor. During the visit of the Azerbaijani defence minister, S. Abiyev, to Ukraine in October 2000 it was reported that a document on the establishment of such a joint unit was being prepared. However, two months later, the deputy defence minister of Georgia, G. Bezhuashvili, said that Tbilisi had no plans to establish a military unit within the framework of the informal forum.[27] As for Moldova and Uzbekistan, from the beginning neither showed much interest in the project. By early 2001, the idea of establishing such a joint GUUAM unit appeared to have been shelved; during the June 2001 meeting of the Council of Ministers of Defence of South-East European Countries in Thessaloniki, the Ukrainian defence minister said that Ukraine had no military interests within the GUUAM framework of activity.[28]

[26] Deputy foreign minister of Ukraine I. Kharchenko said: 'We believe that within GUUAM, prospects for military cooperation exist, first and foremost, on a bilateral basis. The ideas and events discussed by defence agencies fit into the existing plans of military cooperation'. See RFE/RL, Ukrainian service, 14 March 2001.

[27] See Versii Agency, 9 Dec. 2000, *http://www.versii.com*.

[28] See Database of the Centre for Army, Conversion and Disarmament Studies, *http://www.defence-ua.com*.

The disintegration of plans to establish a joint military unit of GUUAM may be explained by three factors. First, there are no clearly formulated military tasks that require consolidated efforts by the member states. Moreover, the development of the oil transport corridor that was the subject of the proposed protection is not yet conclusively decided on, and some of the GUUAM member states might not take part in that project at all. Second, the GUUAM member states lack sufficient resources to maintain the joint unit envisaged – their funds are not enough even for combat training of their regular armed forces. Third, Russian opposition was fairly strong, and the extent of US and NATO support for the idea of the joint unit before 11 September was not significant.

A peacekeeping unit involving two of the GUUAM member states was eventually established, but within the framework of a multinational project. On 2 April 2001 an agreement was signed in Istanbul providing for the formation of a joint naval task force in the Black Sea – BLACKSEAFOR – that united Bulgaria, Georgia, Russia, Romania, Turkey and Ukraine. The main tasks assigned to this force were search and rescue operations, de-mining, humanitarian assistance and environmental protection.[29]

This initiative, advanced in the first instance by Turkey in early 1998, deserves particular attention with regard to its peacekeeping potential. Though still largely symbolic in nature, little publicized, and so far perceived by its participants primarily as a consultative mechanism, it nevertheless establishes a new useful framework for

[29] The force, made up of four to six ships, has already begun to operate. The command will rotate. BLACKSEAFOR may also be used in UN and OSCE peacekeeping and humanitarian operations.

cooperation. This arrangement could have significant potential in the future, especially following changes in regional security priorities after 11 September, including an apparent diminution in Russian opposition to NATO enlargement.

BLACKSEAFOR in fact brought together on equal terms a long-time major opponent to NATO (Russia); a NATO member country (Turkey); NATO candidates and participants in the Membership Action Plan (Bulgaria and Romania); and non-aligned countries that are PfP partners (Georgia and Ukraine). The commander of the Russian Black Sea Fleet, Admiral Vladimir Komoyedov, noted after the conclusion of the formal agreement on BLACKSEAFOR: 'To military professionals, especially neighbours, it is indeed not that difficult to find a common language when discussing the issues of maintaining security and providing support.'[30]

In developing a new framework for better understanding and the interoperability of their navies through BLACKSEAFOR, six Black Sea countries thus embarked on an initiative to develop operational skills that could be applied in many peacekeeping scenarios, where multinational naval patrols, the escort of convoys, the security of supply routes, the management of refugee flows, etc. may be involved. These are routine missions in cases where operations involve both peacekeeping and humanitarian tasks. The Georgian defence minister, Lieutenant-General David Tevzadze, specified that 'When directed by the Foreign/Defence Ministers or their authorized

---

[30] See S. Ukhanev, 'Friendly step towards each other', 21 April 2001, *redstar@mail.cnt.ru.*

representatives, the Force may conduct Peace Support Operations in support of United Nations Security Council and OSCE Resolutions, as well as operations against smuggling, organized crime and terrorism.'[31] The significance of BLACKSEAFOR is likely to grow in view of its potential for possible participation in multinational preventive deployment forces under the auspices of the UN or OSCE in future humanitarian crises.

In September–October 2001 BLACKSEAFOR conducted its first real exercise, when six combat vessels of participating countries embarked on a three-week tour of exercises and port visits around the Black Sea; and by 2002 the command and organizational structure of the force had been completed. Ukraine, which assumed command of BLACKSEAFOR in 2002 (under the annual rotating command system), has actively supported the initiative as an important expression of regional security cooperation. Ukraine expects that BLACKSEAFOR will contribute in particular to the improvement of the international image of Ukraine and its standing as a sea power; will increase the influence of Ukraine on developments in maritime policies in the region; and will improve the Ukrainian navy's readiness to participate in humanitarian and peacekeeping operations.[32]

[31] See statement by Lt-Gen. David Tevzadze, minister of defence of Georgia, at EAPC defence ministers' meeting, NATO HQ, Brussels, 8 June 2001, *www.nato.int*.
[32] See deputy chief of Ukraine's general staff Department for Military Cooperation and Verification, Col. Leonid Holopatiuk, 'Role of combined naval forces in the Black Sea', presentation to international seminar held by the Royal Institute of International Affairs (London) and the National Institute of Security Studies (Ukraine) in Kiev on 18–20 March 2001.

As far as GUUAM is concerned, the NATO PfP programme has resulted in more interaction among the heads of military agencies and personnel of the GUUAM armies than any military initiatives of GUUAM as a military grouping. Since GUUAM was first formed, only two exercises have been held that were prepared with the active participation of Ukraine and completely funded by the member states: the exercise South-98, which involved units of the Ukrainian and Moldovan armed forces, and a trilateral Ukrainian–Azeri–Georgian exercise held in April 1999 on the Yalgudszha range in Georgia.

In contrast, units of the GUUAM member states regularly participate in the traditional annual Peace Shield exercises held in Ukraine within the framework of the PfP programme with financial assistance from the United States, as well as in the annual PfP Cooperative Partner exercise in the Black Sea. Georgia also joined the Ukraine–US exercise Sea Breeze held 'in the spirit of PfP'. NATO did not support the idea of establishing a mechanism of interaction in a 'NATO + GUUAM' format, which was proposed by Ukraine in 2000. NATO was cautious about the establishment of such separate groups, not wanting to create a precedent by segmenting ties with the EAPC partners, since that organization operated on the basis of the equality of all member states in their dialogue with NATO. The alliance believed that issues tackled in the format of GUUAM could be presented by one state, say, Ukraine, either in the format '19 + 1', or in the format of the NATO–Ukraine Commission.[33]

<hr>

[33] S. Zhurets, '"The Tridental Eagle", or on military parallels from the life of strategic partners', *Den*, 12 April 2000.

After 11 September the issue of security cooperation within GUUAM was revived, albeit in a format such as the autumn 2001 session of the UN General Assembly in New York, where foreign ministers of the GUUAM countries discussed the issue of pipeline security and the creation of appropriate structures for this purpose.[34] During a visit by the US Secretary of Defense Donald Rumsfeld to Georgia, Azerbaijan and Uzbekistan in December 2001, it appeared that the United States was firmly behind GUUAM's developing new momentum in pursuing a joint security agenda.[35] Rumsfeld expressed the US desire to develop further cooperation in the areas of military-to-military contacts, fighting terrorism and the overall strengthening of the national security of the three countries he visited.

Despite all the impediments faced by GUUAM, the need to strengthen this grouping is conditioned by the common interests of the member states in securing regional stability, the imperative for deepening trade and economic relations and the implementation of transport and communication projects, and the desirability of maintaining common positions in international organizations.

During the GUUAM summit in July 2002 (again in Yalta), numerous declarations about security were made. The final communiqué signed by the heads of state of

[34] S. Stepanenko, A. Useinov and I. Maksimov, 'Senior brother – for choice. America again offers support to Russia's neighbours', *Vremia Novostey*, 30 Nov. 2001.
[35] See V. Socor, 'Azerbaijan, Georgia, Armenia discuss their antiterror role with Rumsfeld', *Jamestown Foundation Monitor*, vol. 7, no. 231, 17 Dec. 2001.

Azerbaijan, Georgia, Moldova and Ukraine (Uzbekistan did not participate in the summit) confirmed their commitment to combating terrorism and organized crime and 'the necessity of preventing any actions directed at supporting separatist and extremist forces as well as undermining the sovereignty and territorial integrity of GUUAM members'. A declaration was also issued on 'general efforts to maintain stability and security in the region'. As the Ukrainian foreign minister Anatoly Zlenko stated, 'There was almost no dimension of security cooperation within GUUAM, but now it exists.'[36]

The existing security problems in the region and the future realization of large-scale joint economic, energy and transport projects create an objective necessity for joint security measures, maybe even with military means. Despite strong Russian objections, GUUAM member countries could reinvigorate their stalled attempts to form their own security and peacekeeping arrangements,[37] most likely within the framework of the NATO PfP programme. Recent events connected with the threat of international terrorism confirm the view that there exist presently common threats of a military character that could prompt the GUUAM member states to pool efforts in the defence field, particularly in developing capabilities for peacekeeping operations.

[36] See 'Pain points of GUUAM. 1. Security', *http://www.defence-ua.com*, *Defense-Express*, 22 July 2002.
[37] See T. Kuzio, 'The role of GUUAM in the international anti-terrorist strategy', *Eurasia Insight*, 30 Oct. 2001.

5   GENERAL CONCLUSIONS

Cooperation between Ukraine and NATO is gradually improving and broadening. The preservation of Ukraine's sovereignty and independence, and continuing cooperation between NATO and Ukraine, are in NATO's interests, and certainly serve the interests of the Ukrainian people. However, there is an evident need for better promotion of knowledge and understanding of NATO among Ukrainians, who are at present much more familiar with the Russian perspectives, due to the wide availability of Russian newspapers and other media in Ukraine and the scarcity of their Western counterparts.

During 2000–1 the Ukrainian leadership increased the number of friendly gestures towards Russia, but it did not scale back similar gestures towards NATO, and in May 2002 declared the country's intention to join the alliance in the future. However, the tempo of cooperation between Ukraine and NATO is not likely to change significantly from its current pace of gradual improvement. All previous experience of cooperation between Ukraine and NATO, both within PfP and in practical peacekeeping activities, confirms that NATO should continue its cooperation with Ukraine in the defence area at the same level but with more emphasis on improvements in quality, especially with regard to the interoperability of forces (with emphasis on command and control issues and peacekeeping).

NATO can provide more assistance in developing Ukraine's security concepts and doctrinal publications through staff talks and sharing of information about NATO's procedures. There are good prospects for further deepening military-technical cooperation between Ukraine and NATO, specifically through agreements on the mutual protection of classified information with individual NATO countries (similar to the agreement Ukraine concluded recently with Poland), particularly with the United States, the Czech Republic, the UK, Greece, France, Germany, the Netherlands, Poland, Spain and Turkey, and through exploring non-traditional forms of military-technical cooperation, such as the leasing of weapons systems and military hardware. Ukraine could not only provide services in this way, but also use such cooperation to raise the combat readiness of its armed forces.

It makes good sense to consider ways to engage Ukraine more in peacekeeping activity with NATO forces, for example by increasing financial assistance to combined units (such as the joint Polish–Ukrainian battalion, and the joint Ukrainian–Hungarian–Romanian–Slovakian engineers unit Tisa), and by maintaining positive pressure on the Ukrainian military, for example within the framework of the JWGDR, in order to expedite the development and strengthening of the country's ability to generate significant numbers of coherent peacekeeping contingents.

Events in the Balkans and the existence of situations fraught with the risk of conflict in other European countries provide ample evidence that the danger of a military conflict in Europe persists. Threats to European security are real. If those threats are not removed in a timely fashion, they will constantly provoke new conflicts.

NATO has proved its effectiveness and will remain at the core of the European security architecture for years to come. Despite the uncertainty and contradictions which exist in NATO–EU relations, Ukraine's interests require that the country cooperates actively in the security domain with both organizations, and peacekeeping activities are a means to that end. Future possible EU peacekeeping operations could benefit from Ukraine's contribution, which would capitalize on its current cooperation with NATO.

Although Ukraine's attempts in the 1990s to build a peacekeeping entity within the GUUAM grouping failed, discussions are likely to continue in GUUAM about the ways to provide security for joint endeavours and support peace in member countries.

Despite recent declarations of intent to join NATO by Ukraine, it is premature to discuss the likely future date of Ukraine's accession to the alliance; both sides are not yet prepared for such a step. Ukraine's lack of preparedness and the high cost of such an endeavour are not the only issues; Russian opposition to this scenario could be stronger than its opposition to NATO enlargement in eastern and central Europe, even stronger than in the case of the three Baltic countries. At the same time, the deepening of cooperation between Ukraine and the alliance presents an opportunity to avoid a new division of Europe, and fosters security and stability on the continent. Cooperation with NATO also helps Ukraine to

implement internal reforms and to move towards joining the community of developed European countries.

VLADIMIR PUTIN AND THE EVOLUTION OF RUSSIAN FOREIGN POLICY

Bobo Lo

Paperback ISBN 1-4051-0300-0
Hardback ISBN 1-4051-0299-3

'This is a particularly lucid, well-informed and sensible analysis of Putin's approach to Russian foreign policy which professionals and laymen alike can read with pleasure as well as profit.'
– Sir Rodric Braithwaite, former UK Ambassador to Russia

'A well written and vigorously argued book. It is the best overall assessment to date of Putin's foreign policy.'
– Dr Alex Pravda, Director, Russian and East European Centre, St Antony's College, University of Oxford

'Bobo Lo's insight into the opaque world of Russian foreign policy is unique. The way perceptions and myths mix with pragmatism and cynicism to form Moscow's outlook on the world is a fascinating read, which should remain a standard work in its field for a long time.'
– Konstantin Eggert, BBC Russian Service Bureau Chief in Moscow

Contact jnixey@riia.org

TOWARDS INCLUSIVE EUROPEAN SECURITY

Clelia Rontoyanni

Publication: Summer 2003
Paperback ISBN: 1-4051-0302-7

As the European Security and Defence Policy emerges as a new player in the European security landscape, its capacity to project stability beyond the European Union's borders will very much depend on the quality of its engagement with European non-EU member-states. Russia, Ukraine and Belarus, as direct neighbours of an enlarged EU and key actors in the volatile security space of the former Soviet Union, represent top priorities for an outward-looking ESDP. This book investigates how the Russian, Ukrainian and Belarusian foreign policy communities assess their countries' interaction and dialogue with NATO and the EU on security-related issues and how they propose that relations in this field develop - especially following the establishment of the ESDP.

Contact jnixey@riia.org

THE ROYAL INSTITUTE OF INTERNATIONAL AFFAIRS | Russia and Eurasia Programme

POLAND AND UKRAINE
A strategic partnership in a changing Europe?

Kataryna Wolczuk and Roman Wolczuk

Paperback £15.95 ISBN 1-86203-137-1

'As Europe's centre of gravity moves further east following German unification and EU enlargement, states such as Ukraine and Poland are gaining dramatically in importance. This book shows how these two states were able to overcome a painful historical legacy of mass deportations and killing and become strategic partners, even though at the societal level the rapprochement has been more difficult and protracted. However, this new partnership is now under threat as Poland's accession to the European Union leaves Ukraine in economic and political limbo, separated from Poland and the rest of western Europe by a 'hard' Schengen border. This book not only reveals many important and largely unknown details of Polish-Ukrainian relations but also examines their broader geostrategic implications. This is foreign policy analysis at its best and very useful reading for all students of Europe, post-communist transitions and EU enlargement.'

– Jan Zielonka, Professor of Political Science, European University Institute

Contact pubs@riia.org